TEACHER EDITION

ZANER-BLOSER
Spell It—Write!
Helping Beginning Writers

Karen R. Harris, Ed.D.
Steve Graham, Ed.D.
Jerry Zutell, Ph.D.

J. Richard Gentry, Ph.D.

GRADE K

SOUNDS

PHONICS

LETTERS

SPELLING

Spell It–Write! Classroom Package

Spell It–Write! isn't another basal. It's a whole package of materials that uses literature at kindergarten and first grade to bring literacy to life in your classroom!

See the Difference!

Poetry Builds Phonemic Awareness and Sound-Symbol Awareness

A Student Edition

Literature is the core of *Spell It–Write!* in kindergarten. Each of the 26 units is based on a poem that calls the children's attention to a letter, its sound, and its printed form.

Throughout the book, *My Writing* integrates emergent spelling skills with writing.

For more information, see "A Look at the Student Edition," starting on page Z10.

B Teacher Edition

Easy-to-use teaching suggestions help you guide the children as they use literature to play with sounds and words. A variety of activities helps children tune into phonemic awareness and gain sound-symbol awareness, crucial skills for successful readers and writers.

See "A Look at the Teacher Edition," starting on page Z16.

Manipulatives Engage Young Learners

C Picture-Sort Cards

A complete book of *Picture-Sort Cards* helps students develop phonemic awareness as they identify and match the initial sound in the name of each picture. The pages in the book are perforated so they can easily be made into separate cards, or they can be duplicated and cut apart to provide a "unit pack" of cards for each student.

D Letter Tiles

Letter tiles can be used to help children learn names and form, to reinforce sound-symbol relationships, and to help children see how letters combine to make words. *A packet of 60 letter tiles is included.*

Support Materials Make Teaching Easier

E Teacher Resource Book

Convenient reproducibles provide easy-to-use figures to cut out and color. These figures can stimulate children's response to the literature. Also included is an *Assess and Plan* checklist for qualitative assessment.

F Alphabet Posters

Colorful posters show uppercase and lowercase letters to reinforce sound-symbol awareness.

The *Spell It—Write!* Authors

KAREN R. HARRIS, ED.D.

Dr. Harris is among the pioneers in student self-management in spelling and literacy. She coauthored, with Steve Graham, *Helping Young Writers Master the Craft: Strategy Instruction and Self-Regulation in the Writing Process* (Brookline Books, 1992). She is also the coeditor of the book *Promoting Academic Competence and Literacy in School* (Academic Press, 1992).

A member of the College of Education faculty at the University of Maryland, she has also done extensive research and authored numerous articles and chapters on effective strategy instruction and self-management in schools.

STEVE GRAHAM, ED.D.

Dr. Graham is well-known for his research and writing on spelling and literacy, especially in the areas of process-oriented instruction and self-regulation. Dr. Graham's research into the most frequently used words in children's reading and writing led to the development of "The Basic Spelling Vocabulary." This list is the core of the word lists in *Spell It—Write!*

A member of the College of Education faculty at the University of Maryland, Dr. Graham is the coauthor of *Helping Young Writers Master the Craft: Strategy Instruction and Self-Regulation in the Writing Process* (Brookline Books, 1992).

JERRY ZUTELL, PH.D.

Dr. Zutell has done extensive development on the implementation of word sorts and word webs as a way to help students internalize relationships between word sound, structure, and meaning.

A member of The Ohio State University faculty, Dr. Zutell has edited several volumes on literacy and authored numerous articles on spelling, among them "An Integrated View of Word Knowledge: Correlational Studies of the Relationships Among Spelling, Reading, and Conceptual Development," in *Development of Orthographic Knowledge and the Foundations of Literacy* (Lawrence Earlbaum Associates, 1992).

J. RICHARD GENTRY, PH.D.

Dr. Gentry is well-known for his research and writing on invented spelling, process-oriented spelling instruction, and the spelling/writing connection. His books—*Spel...Is a Four-Letter Word* (Heinemann, 1987), and *Teaching Kids to Spell,* coauthored with Jean Gillet (Heinemann, 1992)—are landmark texts for teachers seeking practical techniques for handling spelling instruction in today's classroom.

Dr. Gentry is a member of the Elementary Education Department at Western Carolina University and a former director of the university's reading center.

Stages of Spelling Development

Learning to spell is a developmental process. Researchers have noted that as children move through the process, they pass through five developmental stages. On their way, they are likely to produce spellings characteristic of more than one stage. While this is normal, the stage that describes most of their invented spellings represents their developmental level.

STAGE 1

PRECOMMUNICATIVE

The child spells in random "letter strings" and is aware that letters are symbols. However, the child lacks understanding of the letter-sound correspondence. Example: DLKRODLH spells **elephant**.

STAGE 2

SEMIPHONETIC

The child is aware that letters represent sounds but depends primarily on dominant consonants and letter names to provide the symbols that guide the spellings he or she produces. Example: MBEWWMLnt (My baby was with me last night.)

STAGE 3

PHONETIC

The child is able to break a word into phonemes and then attempts to represent those phonemes with appropriate letters. Example: It trd in to a brd. (It turned into a bird.)

STAGE 4

TRANSITIONAL

The child begins to write words in a more conventional way as he or she moves away from dependence on sound to more reliance on visual memory of how the word looks in print. Example: It turned in too a berd. (It turned into a bird.)

STAGE 5

CONVENTIONAL (CORRECT)

Conventional spelling develops after a number of years of spelling study.

Stages of Spelling Development

Understanding where individual children are developmentally helps the teacher facilitate spelling growth. A good place to begin to gain a better understanding of an individual child's place in that process is to administer this spelling test developed by *Spell It—Write!* author J. Richard Gentry, Ph.D. (from *Teaching Kids to Spell*. J. Richard Gentry and Jean Wallace Gillet. Heinemann Press, 1993).

Gentry advises teachers to follow these directions in administering the test below:

▶ Explain that the words you are going to read may be difficult. Tell the children to invent a spelling for each word or write their best guess.

▶ Explain that the activity will not be graded but will help you understand where each child is as a speller.

▶ Say each word; read the sentence; say the word again.

1.	monster	The monster was in the movie.
2.	united	You live in the United States.
3.	dress	The girl wore a new dress.
4.	bottom	A big fish lives at the bottom of the lake.
5.	hiked	We hiked to the top of the mountain.
6.	human	Miss Piggy is not a human.
7.	eagle	An eagle is a powerful bird.
8.	closed	The little girl closed the door.
9.	bumped	The boy bumped into the table.
10.	type	Type the letter on the typewriter.

The following chart of representative spellings can help teachers analyze children's responses to the developmental spelling test. (Note: Because precommunicative spellings are usually strings of random letters, sample precommunicative spellings are not included on this chart.)

Words	Semiphonetic	Phonetic	Transitional	Conventional
monster	mtr	mostr	monstur	monster
united	u	unitd	younighted	united
dress	jrs	jras	dres	dress
bottom	bt	bodm	bottum	bottom
hiked	h	hikt	hicked	hiked
human	um	humn	humun	human
eagle	el	egl	egul	eagle
closed	kd	klosd	clossed	closed
bumped	b	bopt	bumpped	bumped
type	tp	tip	tipe	type

Literature forms the core of *Spell It–Write!* in kindergarten. Through nursery rhymes and poems, young children play with the sounds, letters, words, and ideas that are the foundation of literacy.

Each unit presents, in a nursery rhyme or poem, a letter of the alphabet and its most common sound-letter correspondence.

Opportunities are provided in every unit for associating sounds and letters, practicing letter formation, and engaging in personal writing.

Temporary spelling is encouraged as a means of developing self-expression and emergent spelling skills.

Six strands guide instruction in all 26 units of kindergarten *Spell It—Write!*

 PHONEMIC AWARENESS

A **phoneme** is a sound within a language. The phoneme English speakers write as **v** is pronounced \v\. So **phonemic awareness** is an awareness of the sounds within a language. A more sophisticated definition is "the ability to examine language independently of meaning and to manipulate its component sounds." (Griffith and Olson 1992)

Basic phonemic awareness includes the ability to recognize rhyming words. A more advanced task is "syllable splitting": identifying the first sound in **cat** as \k\, the middle sound as \a\, and the final sound as \t\. Other phonemic awareness tasks include adding a phoneme to a word and stating the new word: add \k\ to \at\ and say **cat**.

 SOUND-SYMBOL AWARENESS

Sound-symbol awareness is an understanding of the specific letters that represent different spoken sounds: \b\ is written **b**; \d\ is written **d**. Invented spelling is one way children try to relate the sound system they hear to the letter system they see in the environment. While children should be held responsible for spelling conventionally the words they know and write often, invented spelling helps young children develop sound-symbol awareness.

 DICTIONARY SKILLS

Young children generally do not use dictionaries to verify spellings and meanings, but they can become familiar with dictionary structure and alphabetical order by making a picture dictionary. They can also begin to consult the environment (wall charts, bulletin boards, signs) for the conventional spelling of words they want to use in their writing.

 INTERACTIVE WRITING

Spelling is a tool for writing. **Interactive writing** within *Spell It—Write!* is an extension of modeled writing. During interactive writing activities, you and the children work together on the form, content, and conventions of writing. These conventions include writing left-to-right and putting adequate space between words.

 PERSONAL WRITING

Personal writing activities, featured in each *Spell It—Write!* unit, help children become active writers. After all, spelling is for writing.

 SPELLING CONSCIOUSNESS

As children grow as writers, their awareness of spelling in writing will develop into a **spelling consciousness**. This consciousness will help guide their development as conventional spellers.

REFERENCES

Gentry, J.R. *Spel...Is a Four-Letter Word.* Portsmouth, NH: Heinemann Educational Books, 1987, p. 19.

———. "You Can Analyze Developmental Spelling." *Teaching K-8,* Vol. 15, No. 9 (1985), pp. 44–45.

———, and Jean W. Gillet. *Teaching Kids to Spell.* Portsmouth, NH: Heinemann Educational Books, 1993.

Griffith, Priscilla L., and Mary W. Olson. "Phonemic Awareness Helps Beginning Readers Break the Code." *The Reading Teacher,* Vol. 45, No. 7 (March 1992), pp. 516–523.

Temple, C.A., R.G. Nathan, and N.A. Burris. *The Beginning of Writing.* Boston: Allyn and Bacon, 1988.

Letters and sounds are presented in the context of nursery rhymes and poems that are fun for children to listen to and repeat.

W w

Wee Willie Winkie

Wee Willie Winkie runs through the town,
Upstairs and downstairs, in his nightgown;
Rapping at the window, crying through the lock,
"Are the children in their beds?
Now it's eight o'clock."

136   Unit 23

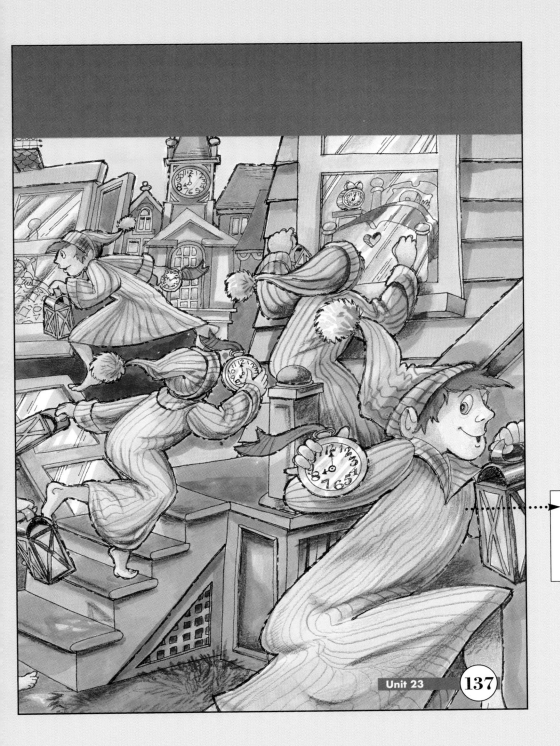

Unit 23 137

Colorful illustrations in a variety of styles help children visualize text.

A Look at the Student Edition

Uppercase and lowercase letter forms help children associate sounds with letters.

Individual Picture-Sort Cards (included in the *Picture-Sort Card Book*) are keyed to the illustrations within each unit's "busy picture." Students gain practice in matching different pictures of the same concept (e.g., a toy **wagon** and a horse-drawn **wagon**) and can manipulate and sort pictures by initial sounds.

138   Unit 23

Children enhance their phonemic awareness and sound-symbol awareness as they search for items whose names begin with the letter/sound targeted in the unit.

FYI Because children may perceive pictured items differently, the teacher should accept alternate labels for items in the busy picture. For example, a picture of a **watch** might also be identified as a **wristwatch**.

Children compile their own picture dictionaries by drawing or pasting appropriate pictures for each letter on the ABC pages at the end of the book.

Letters and Words

Letters and Words provides opportunities for children to practice letter formation and to write words using invented or conventional spelling. Children who are not yet ready for writing may use this page to draw pictures related to the unit's letter/sound.

Letters and Words

W w

My Writing

My Writing

If children understand that spelling is for writing, their spelling consciousness can be nurtured. *My Writing* provides space for children to respond in writing to a theme or topic related to the letter-sound relationship presented in the unit and to move from interactive writing with the teacher to independent personal writing.

A Look at the Teacher Edition

Unit goals and materials are stated at the start of each unit.

PHONEMIC AWARENESS
Symbols clearly identify the purpose of classroom activities.

Suggestions for sharing the literature enhance enjoyment and understanding for children.

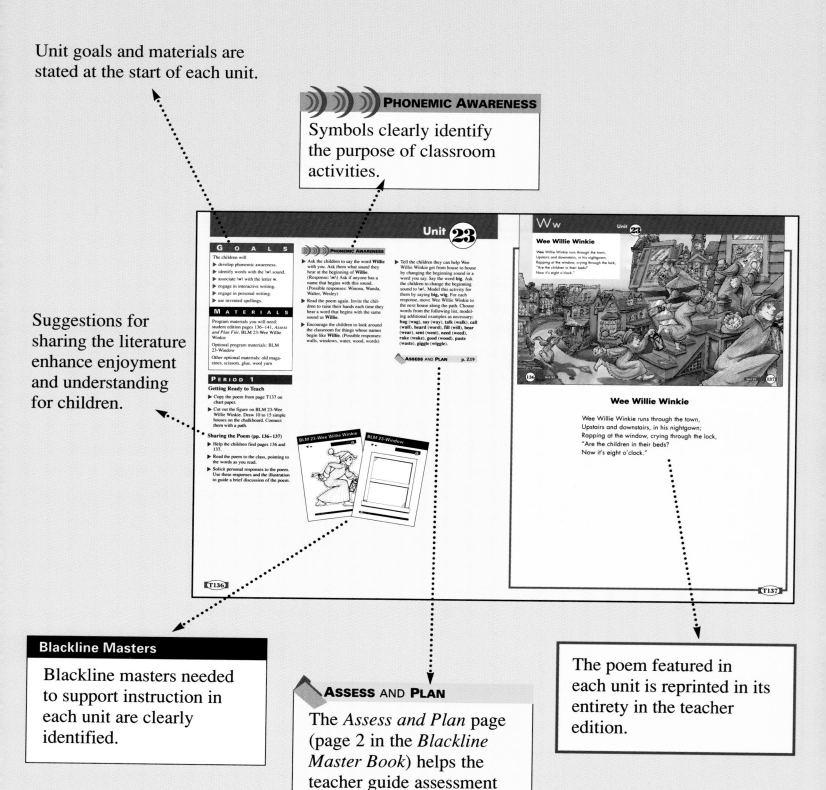

Blackline Masters
Blackline masters needed to support instruction in each unit are clearly identified.

ASSESS AND PLAN
The *Assess and Plan* page (page 2 in the *Blackline Master Book*) helps the teacher guide assessment and plan instruction.

The poem featured in each unit is reprinted in its entirety in the teacher edition.

Concise teaching notes help the teacher introduce new spelling practice activities.

Easy, "doable" teaching suggestions help make content accessible to children whose primary language is not English.

Picture-Sort Cards are available for each kindergarten unit. These cards help build concept awareness and encourage oral language as children match the cards to the individual illustrations in the "busy picture." After two units are discussed, cards from different units can be sorted to reinforce phonemic awareness.

Diversity is a part of our world. These notes by linguist and education specialist Richard Lutz, Ph.D., help the teacher understand dialect differences and the perspectives of all students.

A Look at the Teacher Edition

Letters and Words

Teaching suggestions provide for individualizing instruction and practice.

My Writing

The teacher decides how *My Writing* will enhance spelling development from a menu of *Personal Writing Activities.*

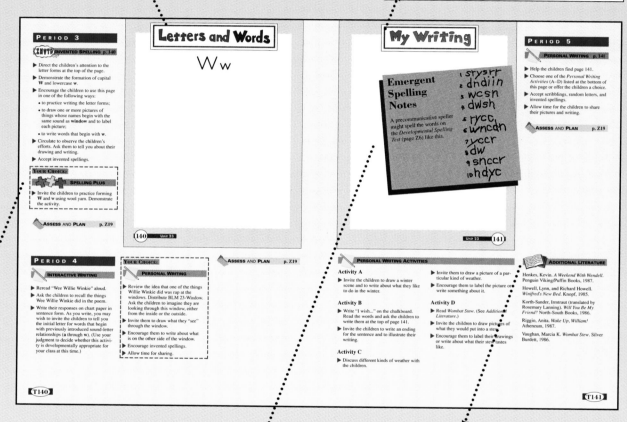

SPELLING PLUS

Spelling Plus provides optional activities. Suggestions for kinesthetic reinforcement are included in all units.

ADDITIONAL LITERATURE

A list of additional resources makes extending themes and spelling concepts easy.

Emergent Spelling Notes

Learning to spell is a process. These notes on emergent spelling by *Spell It—Write!* author J. Richard Gentry, Ph.D., help the teacher use the invented spellings children produce to chart their progress as they move toward conventional spelling.

Assess and Plan, Letter Tiles, Picture-Sort Cards, Phonemic Awareness and Elkonin Boxes

ASSESS AND PLAN

The *Assess and Plan* page (page 2 in the *Teacher Resource Book*) is a quick and easy way to record learners' progress. A clear understanding of each child's development is particularly important in the early years when children are moving through different stages of spelling development. Teachers may wish to refer to the analysis of the *Developmental Spelling Test* (page Z7 in the teacher edition) and the *Emergent Spelling Notes* in each unit to gain additional insight into the children's progress.

To use *Assess and Plan* to greatest advantage, the teacher should make one copy of the *Assess and Plan* page for each child in the class. (*Assess and Plan* can be completed weekly or at other regular intervals throughout the school year.) The completed page documents information helpful for individualizing instruction. Completed *Assess and Plan* pages are also useful in guiding conferences with individual children or with parents.

LETTER TILES

Sixty letter tiles are included in the *Spell It–Write!* Classroom Package for kindergarten. These letter tiles can be used in a variety of ways.

▶ When working with a small group, the teacher can display an individual tile and ask volunteers to identify the sound represented by that letter.

▶ The teacher may arrange tiles to represent responses to activities included in the student edition. The children can then copy the words into their books.

▶ Pairs or small groups of children may work together to arrange tiles to form words they see in the classroom.

▶ The teacher can display tiles for several different letters and pronounce a word that begins with a single vowel or consonant sound represented by one of the letters. Volunteers can find the letter that stands for the beginning sound. For children who are ready, this activity could also be used with ending sounds and letters.

PICTURE-SORT CARDS

A set of *Picture-Sort Cards* is provided for each unit. You may wish to use the set provided (separating the cards along the perforations), or you may wish to duplicate each page of *Picture-Sort Cards* to create multiple sets of cards for your students.

The *Picture-Sort Cards* provided for each unit correspond to individual items included in the "busy picture" for each unit. However, the pictures on the cards have been rendered in a different artistic style and vary—from the illustration in the busy picture—in their portrayal of the targeted word. These differences will enable students to match the concept portrayed in corresponding pictures instead of simply matching identical pictures. On the back of each *Picture-Sort Card*, the initial letter of the pictured item is represented in both upper- and lowercase. For suggestions on using the *Picture-Sort Cards* with your students, see the *Picture-Sort Card Book*.

PHONEMIC AWARENESS AND ELKONIN BOXES

A reproducible page of Elkonin boxes (page 1 in the *Teacher Resource Book*) is included to help build phonemic awareness.

Begin by modeling the use of the boxes. On the chalkboard, draw two boxes like the boxes labelled "2 Sounds" on the Elkonin boxes page. Write "2 Sounds" below the boxes. Tell the children that each box represents one sound in a word.

Say the word **at** aloud. Ask the children how many sounds they hear in this word. Guide them to realize that the word has two sounds, \a\ and \t\. It is not important that the children identify the sounds (e.g., **short a**), only that they realize the word is made of two different sounds.

Say **at** again. As you say \a\, tape a paper circle (or use magnetic markers, if possible) in the first box. As you say \t\, place a marker in the second box.

Now say the word **as** aloud. Ask the students which sound changed, the first sound or the second sound. (Response: the second sound) Move the marker in the second box to demonstrate that change.

Repeat the procedure with a variety of words with two sounds, e.g., **am, all, add, an**.

Duplicate and distribute copies of the Elkonin boxes sheet (*Teacher Resource Book* page 1) to the children. Make sure the students have at least four markers (buttons, etc.). They should always begin with their markers in the large circle and then place one marker in each box as they identify the number of sounds in the words you say. As the children become more adept, you may wish to isolate a single sound and ask the children to move the marker that represents the single sound, e.g., "Move the marker that stands for the sound \t\ in **at**."

If you choose to do activities with Elkonin boxes regularly, you may wish to draw on the words suggested in the *Phonemic Awareness* activity on the first page of most units.

Developmentally Appropriate Teaching and Assessment

by Dominic F. Gullo, Ph.D.
University of Wisconsin-Milwaukee

Because young children do not fall into neat ability groupings, maintaining flexible teaching strategies and individualizing content are particular challenges. Equally challenging is assessing the information and skills young children have learned. *Spell It—Write!* helps teachers meet each child at his or her developmental level. But for each child to benefit fully from *Spell It—Write!,* it will be useful to keep in mind some general developmental considerations.

Children mature at different rates. The implications of this statement for teaching are never so true as in kindergarten and first grade classrooms. Maturational level affects physical-motor ability, language development, problem-solving ability, ability to attend for long periods of time, eye-hand coordination, and the general ability to use new information meaningfully.

Not all children will be able to meet the same expectations. Some children will be able to form letters very close to a specific model, and some will not. Some children will be able to confine their marking to a designated space such as a box, and some will not. It is important to accept children where they are and not expect everyone to meet predetermined expectations.

Teachers will also observe differences in children's ability to be consistent in sound-letter correspondence. Most children can focus on only one thing at a time. Sound-letter correspondence requires them to recognize a letter and a sound and

match the letter to the sound. While some children will be able to do this readily, many will not be able to coordinate visual with auditory perception. This is not an indication of intelligence but of maturity.

Some children at this age have difficulty with part-whole relationships. They may have difficulty taking words apart or putting them together. For these children, it will be helpful to provide concrete activities before exposing them to abstract sounds and words.

Finally, some children may have difficulty understanding that letters can stand for more than one sound or that the same sound can be represented by more than one letter. Again, this has to do with children's ability to focus perceptually on only one thing at a time.

Children will approach activites in *Spell It—Write!* with vigor and interest, but they will achieve at different rates and with different degrees of proficiency. Teachers need to accept children where they are, work with them from where they are, and take them to where they are capable of going.

In dealing with young children, assessment should take a different tone than it does when dealing with more mature learners. Teachers should consider these general principles when assessing young children's progress as they use *Spell It—Write!*

▶ The child is his/her own benchmark as he/she progresses through the curriculum. The teacher should compare the child to himself or herself and not to the rest of the class.

▶ Assessment is ongoing. The primary purpose of assessment is to inform teaching. If teachers assess children only at the end of a curriculum sequence, the chance to modify content or practice so that children can benefit from the experience is lost.

▶ A variety of informal assessment methods increases the likelihood of accurate assessment. Observation, conversation, and questioning provide opportunities to see children in various situations and at different times to get a true picture of progress.

▶ A folder of children's ongoing work can provide valuable information about development. In the *Spell It—Write!* curriculum, many activities repeat from unit to unit. This repetition provides the opportunity to collect samples of children's work systematically and to see the progress individual children are making as they move through the curriculum. The folder will be helpful in making curriculum decisions for individual children and for sharing information with parents.

The *Assess and Plan* page (page 2 in the *Spell It—Write! Blackline Masters*) is a tool that will help teachers put these four principles of assessment in action.

ZANER-BLOSER
Spell It–Write!
Helping Beginning Writers

Karen R. Harris, Ed.D.   Steve Graham, Ed.D.   Jerry Zutell, Ph.D.

J. Richard Gentry, Ph.D.

Zaner-Bloser, Inc.
Columbus, Ohio

Contributing Author

Richard Lutz, Ph.D.
Adjunct Professor,
Applied Linguistics
Georgetown University
Washington, D.C.

Program Consultants

Delores Block
Language Arts Supervisor
Round Rock, Texas

Allen Cox
Language Arts Supervisor
Fort Worth, Texas

A. John Dalmolin II
Elementary Principal
Phoenix, Arizona

Graciela Farias
Language Arts Supervisor
McAllen, Texas

Gladys Hillman-Jones
Educational Consultant
South Orange, New Jersey

Jean S. Mann
Educational Consultant
Sharon, New Hampshire

Robert McGrattan
Elementary Principal
Asheville, North Carolina

George Mundine
Elementary Principal
Houston, Texas

Fran Norris
Language Arts Director
Conroe, Texas

Patti Pace
Assistant Elementary Principal
Houston, Texas

Loretta Parker
School Services Consultant
Reading Specialist
Corpus Christi, Texas

Terry Ross
Language Arts Supervisor
Round Rock, Texas

Karen Swisher, Ph.D.
Director of Reading
Midland Independent
  School District
Midland, Texas

Grade Level Consultants

María A. Alanis
Chapter I Coordinator
Austin, Texas

Ella Bell
Sixth Grade Teacher
Shenandoah Junction,
  West Virginia

Patricia Boyd
Seventh Grade Teacher
Cheektowaga, New York

Claudia Cornett, Ph.D.
Professor, Education
Wittenberg University
Springfield, Ohio

Deborah S. Daniels
Fifth Grade Teacher
Portsmouth, Virginia

Michele Gagen
Kindergarten Teacher
Columbus, Ohio

Marlene Goodman
Second Grade Teacher
St. John, Indiana

Dominic F. Gullo, Ph.D.
Professor
Early Childhood Education
University of
  Wisconsin-Milwaukee
Milwaukee, Wisconsin

Nancy Hamlet
Reading Specialist
Glendale, Arizona

Beverly Hill
Fourth Grade Teacher
Booneville, Mississippi

Janice T. Jones
Prekindergarten Facilitator
Chicago, Illinois

Denise Larson
Third Grade Teacher
Portland, Oregon

Debra M. Leatherwood
Third Grade Teacher
Candler, North Carolina

Cathy Maloney
Fifth Grade Teacher
Boise, Idaho

Peter Monether
Middle School Teacher
Fitzwilliam, New Hampshire

Cheryl Prescott
First Grade Teacher
Brandon, Florida

Anita Ross
Kindergarten Teacher
Detroit, Michigan

Janet Strong
Eighth Grade Teacher
West Point, Mississippi

Mary Thomas Vallens
Fourth Grade Teacher
Irvine, California

Spanish Language Consultants

Maria M. Corsino Bolander
Houston, Texas

Amalia Hermandez
San Antonio, Texas

Lucy Herrera
Weslaco, Texas

Joan Nieto
Columbus, Ohio

Literature: "Alligator Pie" by Dennis Lee. Copyright © 1974 by Dennis Lee. Reprinted by permission of MGA Agency Inc. "Covers" from *Vacation Time* by Nikki Giovanni. Copyright © 1980 by Nikki Giovanni. Reprinted by permission of William Morrow & Company. "Fish," "The Giggling Gaggling Gaggle of Geese," and "The Yak" from *Zoo Doings* by Jack Prelutsky. Copyright © 1967, 1983 by Jack Prelutsky. Reprinted by permission of Greenwillow Books, a division of William Morrow & Company. "A House Is a House for Me" by Mary Ann Hoberman. Copyright © 1978 by Mary Ann Hoberman. Reprinted by permission of Gina Maccoby Literary Agency. "The Pickety Fence" from *One at a Time* by David McCord. Copyright © 1952 by David McCord. Reprinted by permission of Little, Brown and Company. "Big N" from *Dr. Seuss's ABC* by Dr. Seuss. Copyright © 1963 and renewed 1991 by Audrey S. Geisel and Karl Zobell. Reprinted by permission of Random House, Inc. "Quack, Quack!" from *Oh Say Can You Say* by Dr. Seuss. Copyright © 1979 by Dr. Seuss and A.S. Geisel. Reprinted by permission of Random House, Inc. "Rainy Day" from *All on a Summer's Day* by William Wise. Copyright © 1971 by William Wise. Reprinted by permission of William Wise. "U Is for Umbrellas" from *Time for Poetry* by Phyllis McGinley. "My Zipper Suit" from *Sung Under the Silver Umbrella* by Marie Louise Allen. Reprinted by permission of M.L. Allen and the Association for Childhood Education International, 11501 Georgia Avenue, Suite 315, Wheaton, MD. Copyright © 1962 by the Association.

Design: Brock Waldron, Bill Smith Studio

Illustrations: Shirley Beckes, Jessica Clerk, Susan Detrich, Nate Evans, Liisa Chauncy Guida, Steve Henry, Ron Le Hew, Laura Rader, Brian Schatell, Jackie Snider, Peggy Tagel, Toni Teevin, Arnie Ten. Logos by Brock Waldron. Cover art by Theo Rudnak.

ISBN: 0-88085-383-2

Copyright © 1998 Zaner-Bloser, Inc.

Zaner-Bloser, Inc., P.O. Box 16764, Columbus, Ohio 43216-6764 (1-800-421-3018)

Printed in the United States of America

TABLE OF CONTENTS

G O A L S

The children will

▶ develop phonemic awareness.

▶ identify words with the **short a** sound.

▶ associate the **short a** sound with the letter **a**.

▶ engage in interactive writing.

▶ engage in personal writing.

▶ use invented spellings.

M A T E R I A L S

Program materials you will need: student edition pages 4–9, *Assess and Plan File*

Other materials you will need: a photograph of an alligator, green construction paper

Optional materials: old magazines, scissors, glue, aluminum foil

P E R I O D 1

Getting Ready to Teach

▶ Copy the poem from page T5 on chart paper.

▶ Cut a circle from green construction paper; then cut the circle into eight wedges.

Sharing the Poem (pp. 4–5)

▶ Help the children find pages 4 and 5.

▶ Read the poem to the class, pointing to the words as you read.

▶ Solicit personal responses to the poem. Use these responses and the illustration to guide a brief discussion of the poem.

▶ Show a photograph of an alligator. Ask the children how the photograph is different from the pictures in their books. Invite the children to share their knowledge of alligators.

PHONEMIC AWARENESS

▶ Ask the children to say the word **alligator** with you. Ask them what sound they hear at the beginning of **alligator**. (Response: \a\) Ask if anyone has a name that begins with this sound. (Possible responses: Ann, Adam, Albert, Angela)

FYI Some children's names, such as April, Audrey, Aaron, and Amanda, may begin with the letter **A** but not the **short a** sound. Accept these responses, but explain the difference in sound.

▶ Read the poem again. Invite the children to clap to the rhythm as you read.

▶ Invite the children to help you make an alligator pie. Show them the pie pieces you cut out earlier.

▶ Explain the concept of slow motion. Show the children a movement, such as walking, in slow motion.

▶ Tell them you will say a word in slow motion and you want them to say the word in a normal way. For example, if you say **cat** as \k\-\a\-\t\, the children should respond "cat." Each time they say a word correctly, attach a piece of the alligator pie to the chalkboard. Continue the activity until all the pieces of the pie are in place.

▶ Use words that have a **short a** sound and only two or three phonemes, such as **am, at, man, ran, sat, Pam, Jan, bag, hat, sat, pat, dad, cap, tag, wag.**

◤ **ASSESS** AND **PLAN**   p. Z19

Alligator Pie

Alligator pie, alligator pie,
If I don't get some I think I'm gonna die.
Give away the green grass, give away the sky,
But don't give away my alligator pie.

Alligator stew, alligator stew,
If I don't get some I don't know what I'll do.
Give away my furry hat, give away my shoe,
But don't give away my alligator stew.

Alligator soup, alligator soup,
If I don't get some I think I'm gonna droop.
Give away my hockey-stick, give away my hoop,
But don't give away my alligator soup.

—Dennis Lee

Alligator Pie

Alligator pie, alligator pie,
If I don't get some I think I'm gonna die.
Give away the green grass, give away the sky,
But don't give away my alligator pie.

Alligator stew, alligator stew,
If I don't get some I don't know what I'll do.
Give away my furry hat, give away my shoe,
But don't give away my alligator stew.

Alligator soup, alligator soup,
If I don't get some I think I'm gonna droop.
Give away my hockey-stick, give away my hoop,
But don't give away my alligator soup.

—Dennis Lee

SOUND-SYMBOL AWARENESS
(pp. 6–7)

▶ Reread "Alligator Pie" to the class.

▶ Write capital **A** and lowercase **a** on a wall chart. Identify the letter and tell the children it stands for the sound they hear at the beginning of **alligator**.

▶ Ask the children to repeat after you first the sound and then the letter several times: \a\, **a**.

▶ Help the children find pages 6 and 7. Ask them if they can find an alligator in the picture. Write **alligator** under **Aa** on the chart. Ask them what letter begins the word **alligator**. (Response: **a**)

▶ Ask the children to find other things in the picture whose names start with the same sound as **alligator**.

FYI Pictured words are listed at the bottom of the reduced student page.

▶ Prompt the children as needed. At first, you may wish to control the naming of the pictured words. For example, you may ask, *"Do you see an apple?"* and continue in this manner for each pictured word. (Later, the children will become more aggressive in finding picture names independently.)

▶ Write each word on the chart; say the word, emphasizing the **short a** sound; and ask the children to repeat it. Ask what letter begins the word.

▶ Ask the children to generate other words that begin with the same sound as **alligator**. Provide prompts and wait time as needed. Add the children's responses to the wall chart.

6 Unit I

Pictured Words
short a: acrobat, alligator, astronaut, ant, apple, ax, address
long a: acorn, apron, ape

YOUR CHOICE:

 SPELLING PLUS

▶ If you wish to introduce **long a,** write **April** on a wall chart. Say the word and ask the children to repeat it. Ask them what sound they hear at the beginning of **April**. (Response: \ay\) Ask what letter begins the word **April**. (Response: **a**)

▶ Ask the children if they can find anything in the picture on pages 6 and 7 whose name begins with the same sound as **April**. Elicit responses as you did for words beginning with the **short a** sound.

▶ Write each word on the chart; say the word, emphasizing the **long a** sound; and ask the children to repeat it.

▶ Ask the children to generate other words that begin with the same sound as **April**. Provide prompts and wait time as needed. Add responses to the wall chart.

ASSESS AND **PLAN** p. Z19

USING THE PICTURE-SORT CARDS

After the illustrations on pages 6 and 7 have been identified and discussed, consider using the *Picture-Sort Cards* for this unit. For more information on using *Picture-Sort Cards,* see page T12 or the *Picture-Sort Card Book.*

Unit I 7

YOUR CHOICE:

SPELLING PLUS

▶ Help the children find page 160.

▶ Ask them to find the letters **Aa** at the top of the page. Encourage them to draw a picture of something whose name begins with **a** in the space beside the letters, or provide old magazines from which they can cut appropriate pictures to glue beside the letters.

▶ You may wish to review words on the wall chart and suggest the children choose one of these to illustrate.

Diversity in Language and Culture

It is sometimes helpful to understand how individual sounds are made. You may notice that a child is making a sound incorrectly. Knowing something about phonetics—how sounds are produced—may make it easier for you to direct children to produce appropriate sounds.

All languages have consonant sounds and vowel sounds. The chief difference between consonant sounds and vowel sounds is that in pronouncing consonant sounds, air is blocked in some way before it exits the mouth. For example, \p\ is produced by blocking the air at the lips and then releasing it suddenly.

Vowel sounds are produced by vibrating the vocal cords and changing the shape of the tongue and mouth to vary the sound without actually blocking it.

The letter **a** stands for a number of different sounds in English. In **alligator** and **grass,** the tongue is forward and the jaw is lowered: the letter represents a low front vowel. The sound represented by the second **a** in **away** and **alligator** is different in that the jaw is dropped only part way: it is a midfront vowel.

In parts of the southern United States, the **short a** sound may become a diphthong—two vowel sounds—so that **grass** sounds like **gray-us**\.

HELPING STUDENTS ACQUIRING ENGLISH

Use as many of the senses (sight, hearing, touch, taste) as may be appropriate to help students associate objects with vocabulary. For example, the word **apple** may be presented in many ways:

▶ Dip apple halves in paint to make "apple prints."

▶ Use slices of red and green apples to create different patterns.

▶ Plant an apple seed.

▶ Read stories about apples and apple trees to the class.

▶ Taste apples prepared in various ways.

TEMPORARY SPELLING

(p. 8)

▶ Direct the children's attention to the letter forms at the top of the page.

▶ Demonstrate the formation of capital **A** and lowercase **a**.

▶ Encourage the children to use this page in one of the following ways:

- to practice writing the letter forms;

- to draw one or more pictures of things whose names begin with the same sound as **alligator** and to label each picture;

- to write words that begin with **a**.

▶ Circulate to observe the children's efforts. Ask them to tell you about their drawing and writing.

▶ Accept temporary spellings.

YOUR CHOICE:

 SPELLING PLUS

▶ Invite the children to practice forming **A** and **a** using twisted strips of aluminum foil. Demonstrate the activity.

◤ **ASSESS** AND **PLAN**   p. Z19

Letters and Words

Aa

PERIOD 4

INTERACTIVE WRITING

▶ Reread "Alligator Pie" aloud.

▶ Explain to the children what advice is. Ask them to help you think of some good advice for dealing with alligators. Say, *"Never ask an alligator for..."* and ask the children to repeat the words. Invite them to finish the sentence. Suggest they use words that begin with the same sound as **alligator**.

▶ Write their sentences on the chalkboard, omitting initial **a**. Say each word that should begin with **a** (**ask, an, alligator,** and so on) and ask volunteers to write the missing letter.

YOUR CHOICE:

PERSONAL WRITING

▶ Discuss with the group other kinds of advice that might be useful to children their age. Provide prompts regarding safety issues, such as crossing the street, riding a bike, dealing with strangers, sharing, and so on.

▶ Ask the children to draw a picture showing something an adult has said they should always do or never do. Invite them to write a sentence that explains their picture. Encourage them to use temporary spellings.

▶ Allow time for the children to share their pictures and writing.

◤ **ASSESS** AND **PLAN**   p. Z19

My Writing

Emergent Spelling Notes

Scribbling usually comes before children learn to write the letters of the alphabet.

Unit I   **9**

▶ Help the children find page 9.

▶ Choose one of the *Personal Writing Activities* (A–D) listed at the bottom of this page or offer the children a choice.

▶ Accept scribblings, random letters, and invented spellings.

▶ Allow time for the children to share their pictures and writing.

ASSESS AND **PLAN**   p. Z19

 PERSONAL WRITING ACTIVITIES

Activity A

▶ Invite the children to draw a picture of an alligator and write a story about it.

Activity B

▶ Write the word **Animals** on the chalkboard. Read the word and ask the children to repeat it. Point out that this word begins with the same sound and letter as **alligator**. Ask them to write **Animals** at the top of page 9.

▶ Ask the children to cut pictures of animals from magazines and glue them on page 9.

Activity C

▶ Discuss healthful foods with the children.

▶ Ask them what they think alligator pie is and whether it would be healthful or "junk" food. Ask them to support their opinions.

▶ Invite the children to draw a picture of a food they like that is healthful.

▶ Encourage the children to label their pictures or write something about them.

Activity D

▶ Provide magazines for the children to use to cut out pictures of things whose names contain \a\, as in **alligator,** or \ay\, as in **April**.

▶ Ask the children to glue the pictures on page 9. Encourage them to label their pictures or write something about them.

 ADDITIONAL LITERATURE

Barrett, Judi. *Animals Should Definitely Not Act Like People*. Atheneum, 1980.

Bayer, Jane. *A, My Name Is Alice*. Dial, 1984.

Dragonwagon, Crescent. *Alligator Arrived With Apples: A Potluck Alphabet Feast*. Macmillan, 1987.

Ehlert, Lois. *Eating the Alphabet*. Harcourt Brace Jovanovich, 1989.

Isadora, Rachel. *City Seen From A to Z*. Greenwillow Books, 1983.

Nedobeck, Don. *Nedobeck's Alphabet Book*. Children's Press, 1981.

Sendak, Maurice. *Alligators All Around: An Alphabet*. Harper, 1962.

GOALS

The children will

▶ develop phonemic awareness.

▶ identify words with the \b\ sound.

▶ associate \b\ with the letter **b**.

▶ engage in interactive writing.

▶ engage in personal writing.

▶ use invented spellings.

MATERIALS

Program materials you will need: student edition pages 10–15, *Assess and Plan File*

Optional materials: a small jar with a screw-on lid for each pair of children, a pint of whipping cream or heavy cream, salt, a tablespoon, bread or crackers, plastic knives, old magazines, scissors, glue, dried beans

PERIOD 1

Getting Ready to Teach

▶ Copy the poem from page T11 on chart paper.

Sharing the Poem (pp. 10–11)

▶ Help the children find pages 10 and 11.

▶ Read the poem to the class slowly, pointing to the words as you read.

▶ Solicit personal responses to the poem. Use these responses and the illustration to guide a brief discussion of the poem.

YOUR CHOICE:

SPELLING PLUS

▶ Ask the children if they would like to try to make some butter.

▶ Distribute jars to each pair of children. Put a tablespoon of cream and a pinch of salt in each jar and screw on the lid.

▶ Instruct the children to take turns shaking the jar until the cream turns to butter (about five minutes).

▶ Allow the children to spread their butter on a small piece of bread or a cracker to taste it.

FYI If you do not want children to use knives, spread the butter yourself.

▶ Invite the children to describe the taste of the butter. Write their descriptive words on the chalkboard.

▶ Ask the children to list the equipment, ingredients, and procedures used in making the butter. Write these in three separate columns on chart paper. Use the lists to help the children summarize the activity.

PHONEMIC AWARENESS

▶ Ask the children to say the words **Betty Botter** with you. Ask them what sound they hear at the beginning of **Betty** and **Botter**. (Response: \b\) Ask if anyone has a name that begins with this sound. (Possible responses: Bob, Barbara, Bill, Bonita)

▶ Read the poem again. Invite the children to raise their hands each time they hear a word that begins with the same sound as **Betty** and **Botter**.

▶ Encourage the children to look around the classroom for objects whose names begin like **Betty** and **Botter**. (Possible responses: books, bulletin board, boys, ball, box, buttons)

▶ Pronounce pairs of words and ask the children which one begins like **Betty** and **Botter**. Use word pairs that begin with distinctly different sounds, such as **apple/banana, bus/car, boy/girl, look/book, fox/box**.

▶ For children who have difficulty with this task, pronounce one word at a time and ask if it begins like **Betty** and **Botter**.

ASSESS AND **PLAN**　　　　p. Z19

Betty Botter

Betty Botter bought some butter,
But, she said, this butter's bitter;
If I put it in my batter,
It will make my batter bitter,
But a bit of better butter
Will make my batter better.
So she bought a bit of butter
Better than her bitter butter,
And she put it in her batter,
And it made her batter better,
So 'twas a better Betty Botter
Bought a bit of better butter.

—Anonymous

10 Unit 2

Unit 2 11

Betty Botter

Betty Botter bought some butter,
But, she said, this butter's bitter;
If I put it in my batter,
It will make my batter bitter,
But a bit of better butter
Will make my batter better.
So she bought a bit of butter
Better than her bitter butter,
And she put it in her batter,
And it made her batter better,
So 'twas a better Betty Botter
Bought a bit of better butter.

—Anonymous

SOUND-SYMBOL AWARENESS

(pp. 12–13)

▶ Reread "Betty Botter" to the class.

▶ Write capital **B** and lowercase **b** on a wall chart. Identify the letter and tell the children it stands for the sound they hear at the beginning of **Betty** and **Botter**.

▶ Ask the children to repeat after you first the sound and then the letter several times: \b\, **b**.

▶ Help the children find pages 12 and 13. Ask them if they can find a balloon in the picture. Write **balloon** under **Bb** on the chart. Ask them what letter begins the word **balloon**. (Response: **b**)

▶ Ask the children to find other things in the picture whose names start with the same sound as **balloon**.

FYI Pictured words are listed at the bottom of the reduced student page.

▶ Prompt the children as needed. At first, you may wish to control the naming of the pictured words. For example, you may ask, *"Do you see a book?"* and continue in this manner for each pictured word. (Later, the children will become more aggressive in finding picture names independently.)

▶ Write each word on the chart; say the word, emphasizing the beginning sound; and ask the children to repeat it. Ask what letter begins the word.

▶ Ask the children to generate other words that begin with the same sound as **balloon**. Provide prompts and wait time as needed. Add the children's responses to the wall chart.

ASSESS AND **PLAN** p. Z19

Pictured Words

book, balloon, bear, bee, boat, beach ball, bicycle, banana, bird, butterfly

USING THE PICTURE-SORT CARDS

After the illustrations on pages 12 and 13 have been identified and discussed, consider using the *Picture-Sort Cards* for this unit. Possible activities include the following:

▶ Duplicate the *Picture-Sort Cards* for this unit and separate them. Distribute one set of cards to individuals or small groups. Say each pictured word aloud. Ask each student to place the pointer finger of his/her right hand on a *Picture-Sort Card* and then to place the pointer finger of his/her left hand on the matching picture in the illustration in their book. (Students working in groups can take turns.) Walk around to provide assistance and praise their efforts. Encourage children to talk about the pictures.

▶ Separate the *Picture-Sort Cards* and place them in an envelope in an activity center. Label the envelope with the targeted letter, e.g., **B**. Work with individuals or small groups to match each *Picture-Sort Card* with its corresponding picture in the illustration.

For more information on using *Picture-Sort Cards,* see the *Picture-Sort Card Book.*

YOUR CHOICE:

 **SPELLING PLUS**

▶ Help the children find page 160.

▶ Ask them to find the letters **Bb**. Encourage them to draw a picture of something whose name begins with **b,** or provide old magazines from which they can cut appropriate pictures to glue beside the letters.

▶ You may wish to review words on the wall chart and suggest the children choose one of these to illustrate.

Diversity in Language and Culture

The letter **b** represents a common sound in world languages and stands for one of the first sounds babies produce. Technically, the sound is called a voiced bilabial stop: the lips are closed, air pressure builds in the mouth, the vocal cords start to vibrate, and the lips open, releasing the air suddenly.

One related sound is \p\, which is bilabial but not voiced; that is, the vocal cords don't start vibrating before the air is released. Another related sound is \m\, which is voiced but nasal; the air leaks out through the nose.

These sounds are common, although some languages may not have all three. Arabic, for instance, has \b\, but \p\ really doesn't exist as such. Arabic speakers are likely to pronounce English **plastic** as \bi-las-tik\. Korean \p\ is pronounced \b\ between vowels, but otherwise there is no \b\ sound in Korean and the writing system doesn't distinguish \b\ from \p\. Spanish **b** is between \b\ and \v\: **cabo** (end) is \cah-voh\, with lips not quite closed as the letter **b** is pronounced.

These differences are sometimes transferred to English by new learners of the language.

B is an easy letter for children because the sound it represents is easy to produce and because the letter **b** stands for only one sound. (It is silent in a few words: **lamb, comb,** and **crumb,** for example.)

HELPING STUDENTS ACQUIRING ENGLISH

Ask students how many of the objects pictured on pages 12 and 13 are pronounced with the \b\ sound in their primary language. Spanish-speaking children might mention the following words: **balón (ball); bicicleta (bicycle); banana (banana); barco (boat)**. Other words that contain a \b\ sound but which do not begin with \b\ might also be mentioned: **libro (book); abeja (bee).**

PERIOD 3

 TEMPORARY SPELLING

(p. 14)

▶ Direct the children's attention to the letter forms at the top of the page.

▶ Demonstrate the formation of capital **B** and lowercase **b**.

▶ Encourage the children to use this page in one of the following ways:

- to practice writing the letter forms;
- to draw one or more pictures of things whose names begin with the same sound as **balloon** and to label each picture;
- to write words that begin with **b**.

▶ Circulate to observe the children's efforts. Ask them to tell you about their drawing and writing.

▶ Accept temporary spellings.

YOUR CHOICE:

 SPELLING PLUS

▶ Invite the children to practice forming **B** and **b** using dried beans. Demonstrate the activity.

ASSESS AND **PLAN**   p. Z19

Bb

PERIOD 4

INTERACTIVE WRITING

▶ Reread "Betty Botter" aloud.

▶ Remind the children that Betty Botter needed a bit of better butter so her batter would not be bitter. Ask them what Betty Botter may have done with her batter. (Possible response: bake bread or a cake)

▶ Write "Betty Botter bakes..." on the chalkboard. Ask the children if they can figure out why you used a capital **B** for **Betty** and **Botter**. Explain that people's names are always written with a capital letter at the beginning.

▶ Invite the children to finish the sentence using words that start with \b\. Provide prompts if necessary. (Possible responses: biscuits, bacon, beef, bananas, beets, buns)

▶ Write responses on the chalkboard, omitting initial **b**. Allow volunteers to fill in the missing letter.

YOUR CHOICE:

 PERSONAL WRITING

▶ Ask the children to imagine that Betty Botter is a builder instead of a baker.

▶ Ask them to draw a picture of something Betty Botter might build and to label it or write a sentence about it. Suggest they try to think of an object whose name starts with **b**.

▶ Encourage temporary spellings.

▶ Allow time for sharing.

ASSESS AND **PLAN**   p. Z19

My Writing

Emergent Spelling Notes

This scribbled message on a greeting card is a precursor of invented spelling.

✏️ PERSONAL WRITING   p. 15

▶ Help the children find page 15.

▶ Choose one of the *Personal Writing Activities* (A–D) listed at the bottom of this page or offer the children a choice.

▶ Accept scribblings, random letters, and invented spellings.

▶ Allow time for the children to share their pictures and writing.

ASSESS AND PLAN   p. Z19

✏️ PERSONAL WRITING ACTIVITIES

Activity A

▶ Discuss different kinds of balls used for sports: baseballs, footballs, soccer balls, and so on.

▶ Ask the children to draw, or cut from magazines, pictures of different kinds of balls.

▶ Ask them to label their pictures or write something about them.

Activity B

▶ Ask the children to draw a picture of something from a favorite book.

▶ Encourage them to write something about the picture.

Activity C

▶ Ask the children to draw and label pictures of things they might take to the beach or find at the beach.

Activity D

▶ Ask the children to draw a birthday card.

▶ Encourage them to write a short message on the card.

ADDITIONAL LITERATURE

Carle, Eric. *All About Arthur: An Absolutely Absurd Ape.* Watts, 1974.

Lunn, Carolyn. *A Buzz Is Part of a Bee.* Children's Press, 1990.

Purviance, Susan, and Marcia O'Shell. *Alphabet Annie Announces an All-American Album.* Houghton Mifflin, 1988.

T15

G O A L S

The children will

▶ develop phonemic awareness.

▶ identify words with the \k\ sound.

▶ associate \k\ with the letter **c**.

▶ engage in interactive writing.

▶ engage in personal writing.

▶ use invented spellings.

M A T E R I A L S

Program materials you will need: student edition pages 16–21, *Assess and Plan File*

Optional materials: old magazines, scissors, glue, candy corn

P E R I O D 1

Getting Ready to Teach

▶ Copy the poem from page T17 on chart paper.

Sharing the Poem (pp. 16–17)

▶ Help the children find pages 16 and 17.

▶ Read the poem to the class, pointing to the words as you read.

▶ Solicit personal responses to the poem. Use these responses and the illustration to guide a brief discussion of the poem.

PHONEMIC AWARENESS

▶ Ask the children to say the word **covers** with you. Ask them what sound they hear at the beginning of **covers**. (Response: \k\) Ask if anyone has a name that begins with this sound. (Possible responses: Connie, Kate, Curt, Kevin)

▶ Read the poem again. Invite the children to raise their hands each time they hear a word that begins with the same sound as **covers**.

▶ Encourage the children to look around the classroom for objects whose names begin like **covers**. (Possible responses: cupboard, carpet, collar, colors, computer, corner, cups, curls)

▶ Tell the children they can make new words by adding \k\ to the beginning of words you say. Demonstrate by saying "**Andy, candy**" and asking the children to repeat the words. Use these words: **ache** (**cake**), **up** (**cup**), **are** (**car**), **Earl** (**curl**), **air** (**care**), **ape** (**cape**), **old** (**cold**), **at** (**cat**), **ow** (**cow**), **oats** (**coats**), **age** (**cage**).

▶ **ASSESS** AND **PLAN**　　　p. Z19

Covers

Glass covers windows
      to keep the cold away
Clouds cover the sky
      to make a rainy day

Nighttime covers
      all the things that creep
Blankets cover me
      when I'm asleep

            —Nikki Giovanni

16   Unit 3

Unit 3   17

Covers

Glass covers windows
      to keep the cold away
Clouds cover the sky
      to make a rainy day

Nighttime covers
      all the things that creep
Blankets cover me
      when I'm asleep

            —Nikki Giovanni

SOUND-SYMBOL AWARENESS

(pp. 18–19)

▶ Reread "Covers" to the class.

▶ Write capital **C** and lowercase **c** on a wall chart. Identify the letter and tell the children it stands for the sound they hear at the beginning of **covers**.

▶ Ask the children to repeat after you first the sound and then the letter several times: \k\, **c**.

▶ Help the children find pages 18 and 19. Ask them if they can find a cat in the picture. Write **cat** under **Cc** on the chart. Ask them what letter begins the word **cat**. (Response: **c**)

▶ Ask the children to find other things in the picture whose names start with the same sound as **cat**.

FYI Pictured words are listed at the bottom of the reduced student page.

▶ Prompt the children as needed. At first, you may wish to control the naming of the pictured words. For example, you may ask, *"Do you see a camel?"* and continue in this manner for each pictured word. (Later, the children will become more aggressive in finding picture names independently.)

▶ Write each word on the chart; say the word, emphasizing the beginning sound; and ask the children to repeat it. Ask what letter begins the word.

▶ Ask the children to generate other words that begin with the same sound as **cat**. Provide prompts and wait time as needed. Add the children's responses to the wall chart.

FYI If children name words that begin with **k,** write these words on the wall chart in a separate column and explain that sometimes the \k\ sound is spelled **k**.

ASSESS AND **PLAN** p. Z19

18 Unit 3

Pictured Words

cactus, camel, canoe, castle, caterpillar, cat, cow, camera, coat, cage, candle, carrot, collar, cushion, cup, canary

USING THE PICTURE-SORT CARDS

After the illustrations on pages 18 and 19 have been identified and discussed, consider using the *Picture-Sort Cards* for this unit. Possible activities include the following:

▶ Duplicate the *Picture-Sort Cards* for this unit and separate them. Distribute one set of cards to individuals or small groups. Say each pictured word aloud. Ask each student to place the pointer finger of his/her right hand on a *Picture-Sort Card* and then to place the pointer finger of his/her left hand on the matching picture in the illustration in their book. (Students working in groups can take turns.) Walk around to provide assistance and praise their efforts. Encourage children to talk about the pictures.

▶ Separate the *Picture-Sort Cards* and place them in an envelope in an activity center. Label the envelope with the targeted letter, e.g., **C**. Work with individuals or small groups to match each *Picture-Sort Card* with its corresponding picture in the illustration.

For more information on using *Picture-Sort Cards*, see the *Picture-Sort Card Book.*

Unit 3   19

YOUR CHOICE:

   SPELLING PLUS

▶ Help the children find page 161.

▶ Ask them to find the letters **Cc** at the top of the page. Encourage them to draw a picture of something whose name begins with **c,** or provide old magazines from which they can cut appropriate pictures to glue beside the letters.

▶ You may wish to review words on the wall chart and suggest the children choose one of these to illustrate.

HELPING STUDENTS ACQUIRING ENGLISH

After students have reviewed the pictured words several times, play a game with them. Make a mixed list of words with the "hard" **c** or \k\ sound and words without it (e.g., **cat** and **hat**). Ask the students to stand up. Read the list one word at a time, and ask the students to touch their noses or pat their heads when they hear a word with a \k\ sound. Those who act in response to a word that does not contain \k\ must sit down. Those left standing when the time allotted for the game has ended are the "winners."

Diversity in Language and Culture

Although the letter **c** can represent two sounds in English and the \k\ sound can be spelled in more than one way, this unit presents only the **c** spelling of the \k\ sound.

The \k\ sound belongs to the class of consonants known as "stops" because the air is completely stopped as air pressure builds up in the mouth, and then the blockage is released suddenly, producing a sound. The \b\ sound is also a stop. While \b\ is stopped at the lips, \k\ is stopped further back. The back of the tongue rises and blocks the air at the soft palate (or velum) of the roof of the mouth; \k\ is, therefore,

called a velar stop. Its closest related sound is \g\, which is like \k\ except that the vocal cords are vibrating as the air is being released, while \k\ is voiceless. Babies begin making the \k\ and \g\ sounds early, and the children in your class should not have trouble producing them.

One difference between the \k\ sound in English and the corresponding sound in Spanish, French, and many other languages is that the English \k\ is accompanied by a puff of air (or aspiration). Some non-native English speakers pronounce English \k\ without aspiration, making it sound a bit like \g\.

C c

PERIOD 3

 TEMPORARY SPELLING (p. 20)

▶ Direct the children's attention to the letter forms at the top of the page.

▶ Demonstrate the formation of capital **C** and lowercase **c**.

▶ Encourage the children to use this page in one of the following ways:

- to practice writing the letter forms;

- to draw one or more pictures of things whose names begin with the same sound as **cat** and to label each picture;

- to write words that begin with **c**.

▶ Circulate to observe the children's efforts. Ask them to tell you about their drawing and writing.

▶ Accept temporary spellings.

YOUR CHOICE:

SPELLING PLUS

▶ Invite the children to practice forming **C** and **c** using candy corn. Demonstrate the activity.

 ASSESS AND **PLAN** p. Z19

PERIOD 4

INTERACTIVE WRITING

▶ Reread "Covers" aloud.

▶ Ask the children, *"What can you do with covers?"* Write their responses in complete sentences on the chalkboard.

▶ Encourage the children to think of other kinds of covers than those mentioned in the poem. (Possible responses: hats, umbrellas, coats, lids, doors, roofs, book covers)

▶ Ask the children to find words that begin with **c** in the sentences on the chalkboard.

YOUR CHOICE:

PERSONAL WRITING

▶ You may wish to read *Ira Sleeps Over* by Bernard Waber to introduce this activity.

▶ Discuss with the children different uses for a blanket. (Possible responses: to keep warm, to wrap dolls in, to make a tent, to lie on at the beach, to use as a tablecloth at a picnic)

▶ Explain that some children have a special blanket that makes them feel safe and happy. Ask volunteers to tell about a special stuffed animal, toy, book, or other object they like to keep nearby.

▶ Ask the children to draw a picture of an object that is special to them and to write something that describes the picture.

▶ Encourage temporary spellings.

▶ Allow time for sharing.

 ASSESS AND **PLAN** p. Z19

My Writing

▶ Help the children find page 21.

▶ Choose one of the *Personal Writing Activities* (A–D) listed at the bottom of this page or offer the children a choice.

▶ Accept scribblings, random letters, and invented spellings.

▶ Allow time for the children to share their pictures and writing.

ASSESS AND PLAN   p. Z19

Emergent Spelling Notes

Scribbling and the use of letterlike forms come before the developmental stages of invented spelling.

Unit 3   **21**

PERSONAL WRITING ACTIVITIES

Activity A

▶ Ask the children to draw something using their favorite color.

▶ Encourage them to label their pictures or write something about them.

Activity B

▶ Explain that a career is what adults sometimes call their jobs. Ask the children what careers they know about that they think they might like to do when they grow up.

▶ Ask them to draw pictures showing themselves in their future careers.

▶ Encourage them to write something about their pictures.

Activity C

▶ Ask the children to pretend they are going to make a cake. Ask them to draw a picture showing what they would put into the cake.

▶ Encourage them to write a list of the ingredients for the cake or to write the name of the cake.

Activity D

▶ Ask the children to draw a picture of an animal whose name begins with **c**. (Possibilities include camel, caterpillar, cat, collie, cougar, coyote, cow, calf, colt, cub, canary, cardinal, cobra.)

▶ Encourage them to label the picture and write one fact they know about the animal.

ADDITIONAL LITERATURE

Carle, Eric. *The Very Hungry Caterpillar*. Putnam Publishing Group, 1986.

Freeman, Don. *Corduroy*. Penguin USA, 1968.

Slobodkina, Esphyr. *Caps for Sale*. Harper & Row, 1984.

Waber, Bernard. *Ira Sleeps Over*. Houghton Mifflin, 1973.

G O A L S

The children will

▶ develop phonemic awareness.

▶ identify words with the \d\ sound.

▶ associate \d\ with the letter **d**.

▶ engage in interactive writing.

▶ engage in personal writing.

▶ use invented spellings.

M A T E R I A L S

Program materials you will need: student edition pages 22–27, *Assess and Plan File*

Optional materials: old magazines, scissors, glue, colored construction paper or stick-on circles

P E R I O D 1

Getting Ready to Teach

▶ Copy the poem from page T23 on chart paper.

▶ If you choose the activity under *Your Choice: Spelling Plus* on this page, arrange a visit from someone who plays the violin. The music teacher may know an upper-elementary student who would be willing to play for your class.

Sharing the Poem (pp. 22–23)

▶ Help the children find pages 22 and 23.

▶ Read the poem to the class, pointing to the words as you read.

▶ Solicit personal responses to the poem. Use these responses and the illustration to guide a brief discussion of the poem.

))))))))) PHONEMIC AWARENESS

▶ Ask the children to say the word **dog** with you. Ask them what sound they hear at the beginning of **dog**. (Response: \d\) Ask if anyone has a name that begins with this sound. (Possible responses: Dan, Darleen, Dave, Dana)

▶ Read the poem again. Invite the children to raise their hands each time they hear a word that begins with the same sound as **dog**.

▶ Encourage the children to look around the classroom for objects whose names begin like **dog**. (Possible responses: desk, door)

▶ Tell the children they can make new words by adding \d\ to the beginning of words you say. Demonstrate by saying "**an, Dan**" and asking the children to repeat the words. Use these words: **add** (dad), **ark** (dark), **or** (door), **ear** (dear), **inner** (dinner), **air** (dare), **ash** (dash), **I'm** (dime), **Andy** (dandy), **ate** (date), **ugh** (dug).

┌─────────────────────────────────────┐
YOUR CHOICE:

 SPELLING PLUS

▶ Introduce the violinist to the class. Point out that the player's instrument is called a violin. Ask the children to repeat the word **violin** with you. Tell them a violin is like the fiddle in the poem "Hey, Diddle, Diddle."

▶ Ask the violinist to play a short piece, to describe the instrument and its parts, and to tell how he or she became interested in playing.
└─────────────────────────────────────┘

ASSESS AND **PLAN**   p. Z19

Hey, Diddle, Diddle

Hey, diddle, diddle!
    The cat and the fiddle,
The cow jumped over the moon;
    The little dog laughed
    To see such sport,
And the dish ran away with the spoon.

Hey, Diddle, Diddle

Hey, diddle, diddle!
    The cat and the fiddle,
The cow jumped over the moon;
    The little dog laughed
    To see such sport,
And the dish ran away with the spoon.

SOUND-SYMBOL AWARENESS
(pp. 24–25)

▶ Reread "Hey, Diddle, Diddle" to the class.

▶ Write capital **D** and lowercase **d** on a wall chart. Identify the letter and tell the children it stands for the sound they hear at the beginning of **dog**.

▶ Ask the children to repeat after you first the sound and then the letter several times: \d\, **d**.

▶ Help the children find pages 24 and 25. Ask them if they can find a dog in the picture. Write **dog** under **Dd** on the chart. Ask them what letter begins the word **dog**. (Response: **d**)

▶ Ask the children to find other things in the picture whose names start with the same sound as **dog**.

FYI Pictured words are listed at the bottom of the reduced student page.

▶ Prompt the children as needed. At first, you may wish to control the naming of the pictured words. For example, you may ask, *"Do you see a doll?"* and continue in this manner for each pictured word. (Later, the children will become more aggressive in finding picture names independently.)

▶ Write each word on the chart; say the word, emphasizing the beginning sound; and ask the children to repeat it. Ask what letter begins the word.

▶ Ask the children to generate other words that begin with the same sound as **dog**. Provide prompts and wait time as needed. Add the children's responses to the wall chart.

Pictured Words
doll, dog, dish, daisies, dinosaur, duck, diamond, deer, dollar, donkey, door

 ASSESS AND **PLAN**　　　**p. Z19**

USING THE PICTURE-SORT CARDS

After the illustrations on pages 24 and 25 have been identified and discussed, consider using the *Picture-Sort Cards* for this unit. Possible activities include the following:

▶ Duplicate the *Picture-Sort Cards* for this unit and separate them. Distribute one set of cards to individuals or small groups. Say each pictured word aloud. Ask each student to place the pointer finger of his/her right hand on a *Picture-Sort Card* and then to place the pointer finger of his/her left hand on the matching picture in the illustration in their book. (Students working in groups can take turns.) Walk around to provide assistance and praise their efforts. Encourage children to talk about the pictures.

▶ Separate the *Picture-Sort Cards* and place them in an envelope in an activity center. Label the envelope with the targeted letter, e.g., **D**. Work with individuals or small groups to match each *Picture-Sort Card* with its corresponding picture in the illustration.

For more information on using *Picture-Sort Cards*, see the *Picture-Sort Card Book*.

Unit 4 **25**

YOUR CHOICE:

SPELLING PLUS

► Help the children find page 161.

► Ask them to find the letters **Dd** in the middle of the page. Encourage them to draw a picture of something whose name begins with **d,** or provide old magazines from which they can cut appropriate pictures to glue beside the letters.

► You may wish to review words on the wall chart and suggest the children choose one of these to illustrate.

Diversity in Language and Culture

The letter **d** always represents the same sound—**d**\—in English. Like **b**\ and **k**\, **d**\ is a stop: air is completely blocked in the mouth as air pressure builds up and then is released all at once. While **b**\ blocks the air at the lips and **k**\ blocks the air at the back of the roof of the mouth, **d**\ blocks the air with the tip of the tongue against the bony ridge at the back of the teeth. It is a dental stop. It is voiced, like **b**\, which means the vocal cords are vibrating as the air is released. It is a common sound in languages around the world.

Related to **d**\ is its voiceless counterpart, **t**\. American English speakers tend to pronounce **d**\ and **t**\ the same between vowels, so that **ladder** and **latter** sound the same.

Children begin making the **d**\ sound very early (as in **dada**), and it seldom causes pronunciation problems.

HELPING STUDENTS ACQUIRING ENGLISH

To aid students in acquiring vocabulary, emphasize the use of illustrations (such as the one on pages 24 and 25) and wall charts. Assign each student a study buddy whose primary language is English or who is in a more advanced stage of English acquisition. Ask the study buddy to point to and identify pictured objects in the illustration or chart. The student who is acquiring English should repeat the word. Partners should go over the illustrations several times.

T25

Getting Ready to Teach

▶ If you choose the activity under *Your Choice: Spelling Plus,* cut circles about one-half inch in diameter from colored construction paper (or obtain precut stick-on circles). Provide 20 circles for each child.

 TEMPORARY SPELLING

(p. 26)

▶ Direct the children's attention to the letter forms at the top of the page.

▶ Demonstrate the formation of capital **D** and lowercase **d**.

▶ Encourage the children to use this page in one of the following ways:

- to practice writing the letter forms;
- to draw one or more pictures of things whose names begin with the same sound as **dog** and to label each picture;
- to write words that begin with **d**.

▶ Circulate to observe the children's efforts. Ask them to tell you about their drawing and writing.

▶ Accept temporary spellings.

YOUR CHOICE:

SPELLING PLUS

▶ Invite the children to practice forming **D** and **d** using colored dots (circles). Demonstrate the activity.

ASSESS AND **PLAN**   **p. Z19**

PERIOD 4

 INTERACTIVE WRITING

▶ Reread "Hey, Diddle, Diddle" aloud.

▶ Discuss the make-believe aspects of the poem. Ask questions such as these:

- Can a cat play a fiddle?
- Can a dog laugh?
- Can a dish run away with a spoon?

Letters and Words

D d

▶ Invite the children to think of silly questions using the words **dog** and **dish** or other words that start with \d\. To stimulate their thinking, you might offer a few examples:

- Can a dog dig a ditch?
- Can a dish do a dance?

▶ Write their questions on the chalkboard. Ask the children to find words that start with **d** in these sentences.

YOUR CHOICE:

 PERSONAL WRITING

▶ Invite the children to illustrate one of the sentences on the chalkboard or one of their own. Encourage them to label the drawing or write a sentence about it.

▶ Encourage temporary spellings.

▶ Allow time for sharing.

ASSESS AND **PLAN**   **p. Z19**

My Writing

Emergent Spelling Notes

A precommunicative speller, Leslie produces random letters to describe a flock of butterflies. Leslie does not yet know the alphabetic principle.

Getting Ready to Teach

▶ If you choose Activity B, cut circles about one-half inch in diameter from colored construction paper (or obtain precut stick-on circles). Provide 20 circles for each child.

 PERSONAL WRITING   p. 27

▶ Help the children find page 27.

▶ Choose one of the *Personal Writing Activities* (A–D) listed at the bottom of this page or offer the children a choice.

▶ Accept scribblings, random letters, and invented spellings.

▶ Allow time for the children to share their pictures and writing.

ASSESS AND **PLAN**   p. Z19

PERSONAL WRITING ACTIVITIES

Activity A

▶ Discuss with the children different things they do during the day.

▶ Ask them to draw a picture of one of these activities. Encourage them to label the picture or write something about it.

Activity B

▶ Distribute about 20 colored dots (circles) to each child. Invite the children to use the dots to make a picture.

▶ Encourage the children to label the picture or write a story about it.

Activity C

▶ Open a discussion about doors with the children. Discuss types of doors (glass, wood, metal, revolving, automatic) and their uses (to close off a room, to provide entrances and exits to buildings, to cover cupboards and closets).

▶ Invite the children to draw a picture of a door and write about what is behind the door.

Activity D

▶ Invite the children to share what they know about real and fictional dinosaurs.

▶ Ask them to draw a picture of a real or make-believe dinosaur.

▶ Encourage them to write a fact or a story about the dinosaur picture.

ADDITIONAL LITERATURE

Barton, Byron. *Dinosaurs, Dinosaurs*. Thomas Y. Crowell, 1989.

Saunders, Dave and Julie. *Dibble and Dabble*. Bradbury Press, 1990.

Steig, William. *Dr. De Soto*. Farrar, Straus & Giroux, 1982.

GOALS

The children will

▶ develop phonemic awareness.

▶ identify words with the **short e** sound.

▶ associate the **short e** sound with the letter **e**.

▶ engage in interactive writing.

▶ engage in personal writing.

▶ use invented spellings.

MATERIALS

Program materials you will need: student edition pages 28–33, *Assess and Plan File,* BLM 5-Elephant

Optional materials: old magazines, scissors, glue, elbow macaroni

PERIOD 1

Getting Ready to Teach

▶ Copy the poem from page T29 on chart paper.

▶ Cut out the elephant parts on BLM 5-Elephant.

Sharing the Poem (pp. 28–29)

▶ Help the children find pages 28 and 29.

▶ Read the poem to the class, pointing to the words as you read.

▶ Solicit personal responses to the poem. Use these responses and the illustration to guide a brief discussion of the poem.

▶ Demonstrate the following movements to go with each line of the poem:

- Line 1: Sway from side to side.
- Lines 2 and 3: Loop arms out beside body.
- Line 4: Shake head and wiggle fingers.
- Line 5: Shake head and wiggle feet.
- Line 6: Place nose on shoulder and extend arm.

▶ Invite the children to recite the poem with you, including the actions.

)))))) PHONEMIC AWARENESS

▶ Ask the children to say the word **egg** with you. Ask them what sound they hear at the beginning of **egg**. (Response: \e\) Ask if anyone has a name that begins with this sound. (Possible responses: Ed, Emma, Esther, Everett)

▶ Tell the children you will say a word in slow motion and ask them to say the word in a normal way. For example, if you say **pet** as \p\-\e\-\t\, the children should respond "pet." Each time they say a word correctly, attach a piece of the elephant to the chalkboard, beginning with the body. Continue the activity until all the pieces of the elephant are in place.

▶ Use words that have a **short e** sound and no more than three phonemes, such as **let, men, red, set, met, tell, wet, hen, yes, bell, leg, neck, ten, sell, yet, beg, jet, den**.

◢ **ASSESS** AND **PLAN**   p. Z19

BLM 5-Elephant

The Elephant

The elephant goes like this and that.
He's terrible big.
And he's terrible fat.
He has no fingers.
And he has no toes.
But goodness gracious, what a nose!

The Elephant

The elephant goes like this and that.

He's terrible big.

And he's terrible fat.

He has no fingers.

And he has no toes.

But goodness gracious, what a nose!

SOUND-SYMBOL AWARENESS

(pp. 30–31)

▶ Reread "The Elephant" to the class.

▶ Write capital **E** and lowercase **e** on a wall chart. Identify the letter and tell the children it stands for the sound they hear at the beginning of **egg**.

▶ Ask the children to repeat after you first the sound and then the letter several times: \e\, **e**.

▶ Help the children find pages 30 and 31. Ask them if they can find an egg in the picture. Write **egg** under **Ee** on the chart. Ask them what letter begins the word **egg**. (Response: **e**)

▶ Ask the children to find other things in the picture whose names start with the same sound as **egg**.

FYI Pictured words are listed at the bottom of the reduced student page.

▶ Prompt the children as needed. At first, you may wish to control the naming of the pictured words. For example, you may ask, *"Do you see an elephant?"* and continue in this manner for each pictured word. (Later, the children will become more aggressive in finding picture names independently.)

▶ Write each word on the chart; say the word, emphasizing the **short e** sound; and ask the children to repeat it. Ask what letter begins the word.

▶ Ask the children to generate other words that begin with the same sound as **egg**. Provide prompts and wait time as needed. Add the children's responses to the wall chart.

E e

30 Unit 5

Pictured Words
short e: elephant, escalator, egg, engine, elbow, elf, elk
long e: eagle, easel, eraser

YOUR CHOICE:

 SPELLING PLUS

▶ If you wish to introduce **long e**, write **even** on a wall chart. Say the word and ask the children to repeat it. Ask them what sound they hear at the beginning of **even**. (Response: \ee\) Ask what letter begins the word **even**. (Response: **e**)

▶ Ask the children if they can find anything in the picture on pages 30 and 31 whose name begins with the same sound as **even**. Elicit responses as you did for words beginning with the **short e** sound.

▶ Write each word on the chart; say the word, emphasizing the **long e** sound; and ask the children to repeat it.

▶ Ask the children to generate other words that begin with the same sound as **even**. Provide prompts and wait time as needed. Add responses to the wall chart.

ASSESS AND PLAN p. Z19

USING THE PICTURE-SORT CARDS

After the illustrations on pages 30 and 31 have been identified and discussed, consider using the *Picture-Sort Cards* for this unit. For more information on using *Picture-Sort Cards*, see page T24 or the *Picture-Sort Card Book*.

Unit 5 31

YOUR CHOICE:

SPELLING PLUS

▶ Help the children find page 161.

▶ Ask them to find the letters **Ee.** Encourage them to draw a picture of something whose name begins with **e,** or provide old magazines from which they can cut appropriate pictures to glue beside the letters.

▶ You may wish to review words on the wall chart and suggest the children choose one of these to illustrate.

Diversity in Language and Culture

The letter **e** is used to represent several vowel sounds in English. It is often silent as well. When one symbol, such as **e,** stands for a number of different sounds, it is harder for children to learn to associate the sounds and the symbol.

This unit emphasizes the **short e** sound. Teaching the **long e** sound is optional. The terms **short** and **long** are misleading because the difference between them has nothing to do with how long the sound is sustained but with how much the jaw is dropped in producing the sound. (In Old English, the long vowel sounds actually were held longer than the short vowel sounds.)

The **short e** sound is a mid-front vowel: the jaw is dropped midway, and the tongue is pushed forward. The **long e** sound is a high front tense vowel: the front of the mouth is less open, the tongue is raised and pushed forward, and the tongue muscle is tensed.

Say **met,** then **meet,** holding the vowel sound in each word. You should feel your mouth close a bit and your tongue tense up for **meet.**

In languages around the world, the **long e** sound (high front tense vowel) and the **short e** sound (mid-front lax vowel) are common, though English is unusual in using **e** to represent both sounds.

HELPING STUDENTS ACQUIRING ENGLISH

Both the **short e** and the **long e** sounds exist in other languages, but both are not written using the letter **e.** Information in *Diversity in Language and Culture* (on this teacher page) notes that English is unusual in using **e** to represent both sounds. In Spanish, the **long e** (as in **meet**) is written with the letter **i** or the letter **y.**

Ask Spanish-speaking students to mention several words in their primary language that have the sound of **long e.** Write the words on the chalkboard or ask a parent or Spanish-speaking assistant to do so. Ask students to contrast the ways the sound is written in English and in Spanish. Then ask students to point out the objects in the illustration on pages 30 and 31 that have the **short e** sound in Spanish. Responses include: **elefante (elephant); escalera mecánica (escalator); huevo (egg); elfo (elf).**

TEMPORARY SPELLING

(p. 32)

▶ Direct the children's attention to the letter forms at the top of the page.

▶ Demonstrate the formation of capital **E** and lowercase **e**.

▶ Encourage the children to use this page in one of the following ways:

- to practice writing the letter forms;

- to draw one or more pictures of things whose names begin with the same sound as **egg** and to label each picture;

- to write words that begin with **e**.

▶ Circulate to observe the children's efforts. Ask them to tell you about their drawing and writing.

▶ Accept temporary spellings.

YOUR CHOICE:

 SPELLING PLUS

▶ Invite the children to practice forming **E** and **e** using elbow macaroni. Demonstrate the activity.

◥ **ASSESS** AND **PLAN**   p. Z19

 **Letters and Words**

E e

PERIOD 4

INTERACTIVE WRITING

▶ Reread "The Elephant" aloud.

▶ Ask the children to help you write some sentences about elephants.

- Begin by writing "Every elephant..." on the chalkboard or on chart paper.

- Read the words and ask the children to repeat them with you.

- Ask volunteers to help you finish the sentence so it says something that is true about all elephants. (Possible responses: has a trunk, has two ears, has four legs, has a tail, has to eat, is enormous)

- Write each response as a complete sentence.

YOUR CHOICE:

PERSONAL WRITING

▶ Encourage the children to write another sentence about an elephant, but this time ask them to make it a silly sentence and to include another word that starts with \e\.

▶ You might want to give them some prompts by talking about other words that start with \e\ and discussing their meanings, if necessary. Words you might discuss include **echo, engine, emerald, education, enemy, energy**.

▶ Encourage the children to illustrate their sentences with drawings. You might model this activity by drawing a picture of an elephant in a classroom. Under your drawing, write "Every elephant needs an education."

▶ Encourage temporary spellings.

▶ Allow time for sharing. The children might enjoy concealing their sentences and asking classmates to guess what they have written by looking at the picture.

◥ **ASSESS** AND **PLAN**   p. Z19

My Writing

Emergent Spelling Notes

Encourage story writing. This story, written in semiphonetic spelling, describes a picture of Meredith's father.

DNe
peNr.dre

▶ Help the children find page 33.

▶ Choose one of the *Personal Writing Activities* (A–D) listed at the bottom of this page or offer the children a choice.

▶ Accept scribblings, random letters, and invented spellings.

▶ Allow time for the children to share their pictures and writing.

ASSESS AND **PLAN**   p. Z19

Unit 5   (33)

PERSONAL WRITING ACTIVITIES

Activity A

▶ Invite the children to make up a story about the picture on pages 30 and 31.

Activity B

▶ Discuss electricity with the children and how it is used. Encourage them to name appliances in their homes that use electricity.

▶ Provide old magazines from which they can cut pictures of things that use electricity.

▶ Encourage the children to label their pictures or write something about them.

Activity C

▶ Introduce the word **edible**. Explain that edible things are things that can be eaten.

▶ Ask the children to draw, or cut from magazines, pictures of things that are edible and things that are not edible.

▶ Invite them to use the top half of the page for things that can be eaten and the bottom half for things that cannot be eaten.

▶ Encourage them to label each half of the page or to write a sentence describing each category.

Activity D

▶ Discuss different kinds of exercise, such as walking to school, running a race, and riding a bike.

▶ Ask the children to draw a picture of someone exercising.

▶ Encourage them to label the picture or write something about it.

ADDITIONAL LITERATURE

Griffith, Helen. *Emily and the Enchanted Frog*. Greenwillow Books, 1989.

Hall, Derek. *Elephant Bathes*. Alfred A. Knopf and Sierra Club/Growing Up Books, 1985.

Yolen, Jane. *The Emperor and the Kite*. Philomel Books, 1988.

G O A L S

The children will

▶ develop phonemic awareness.

▶ identify words with the \f\ sound.

▶ associate \f\ with the letter **f**.

▶ engage in interactive writing.

▶ engage in personal writing.

▶ use invented spellings.

M A T E R I A L S

Program materials you will need: student edition pages 34–39, *Assess and Plan File,* BLM 6-Fish

Optional materials: old magazines, scissors, glue, construction paper, finger paint

P E R I O D 1

Getting Ready to Teach

▶ Copy the poem from page T35 on chart paper.

Sharing the Poem (pp. 34–35)

▶ Help the children find pages 34 and 35.

▶ Read the poem to the class, pointing to the words as you read.

▶ Solicit personal responses to the poem. Use these responses and the illustration to guide a brief discussion of the poem.

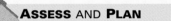

PHONEMIC AWARENESS

▶ Ask the children to say the word **fish** with you. Ask them what sound they hear at the beginning of **fish**. (Response: \f\) Ask if anyone has a name that begins with this sound. (Possible responses: Faith, Felicia, Fred, Frank)

▶ Read the poem again. Invite the children to raise their hands each time they hear a word that begins with the same sound as **fish**.

▶ Encourage the children to look around the classroom for objects whose names begin like **fish**. (Possible responses: faces, feet, fingers, foreheads, floor, furniture, flag)

▶ Pronounce a pair of words and ask the children which word begins like **fish**. Use these pairs or others of your own choosing: **can/fan, fat/bat, fog/dog, car/far, fine/dine, beat/feet, bed/fed, fuzz/buzz, kind/find, fox/box, bun/fun, fill/bill, bit/fit, fell/bell, bin/fin, dare/fair, fear/dear.**

ASSESS AND **PLAN**   p. Z19

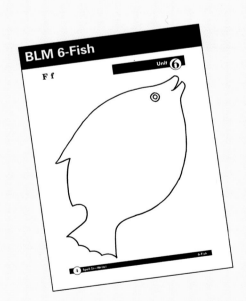

BLM 6-Fish

F f

Fish

Fish have fins
and fish have tails;
fish have skins
concealed by scales.
Fish are seldom
found on land;
fish would rather
swim than stand.

—Jack Prelutsky

Fish

Fish have fins
and fish have tails;
fish have skins
concealed by scales.
Fish are seldom
found on land;
fish would rather
swim than stand.

—Jack Prelutsky

◕)) **SOUND-SYMBOL AWARENESS**

(pp. 36–37)

▶ Reread "Fish" to the class.

▶ Write capital **F** and lowercase **f** on a wall chart. Identify the letter and tell the children it stands for the sound they hear at the beginning of **fish**.

▶ Ask the children to repeat after you first the sound and then the letter several times: \f\, **f**.

▶ Help the children find pages 36 and 37. Ask them if they can find a fish in the picture. Write **fish** under **Ff** on the chart. Ask them what letter begins the word **fish**. (Response: **f**)

▶ Ask the children to find other things in the picture whose names start with the same sound as **fish**.

▷ **FYI** ▷ Pictured words are listed at the bottom of the reduced student page.

▶ Prompt the children as needed. At first, you may wish to control the naming of the pictured words. For example, you may ask, *"Do you see a feather?"* and continue in this manner for each pictured word. (Later, the children will become more aggressive in finding picture names independently.)

▶ Write each word on the chart; say the word, emphasizing the beginning sound; and ask the children to repeat it. Ask what letter begins the word.

▶ Ask the children to generate other words that begin with the same sound as **fish**. Provide prompts and wait time as needed. Add the children's responses to the wall chart.

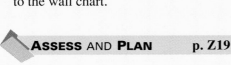 **ASSESS** AND **PLAN** p. Z19

36 Unit 6

Pictured Words
fish, fire fighter, feet, feather, fence, football, five, fork, four, fox, forest

USING THE PICTURE-SORT CARDS

After the illustrations on pages 36 and 37 have been identified and discussed, consider using the *Picture-Sort Cards* for this unit. Possible activities include the following:

▶ Duplicate the *Picture-Sort Cards* for this unit and separate them. Distribute one set of cards to individuals or small groups. Say each pictured word aloud. Ask each student to place the pointer finger of his/her right hand on a *Picture-Sort Card* and then to place the pointer finger of his/her left hand on the matching picture in the illustration in their book. (Students working in groups can take turns.) Walk around to provide assistance and praise their efforts. Encourage children to talk about the pictures.

▶ Separate the *Picture-Sort Cards* and place them in an envelope in an activity center. Label the envelope with the targeted letter, e.g., **F**. Work with individuals or small groups to match each *Picture-Sort Card* with its corresponding picture in the illustration.

For more information on using *Picture-Sort Cards*, see the *Picture-Sort Card Book*.

Unit 6   37

┌─────────────────────────────┐
YOUR CHOICE:

 SPELLING PLUS

▶ Help the children find page 162.

▶ Ask them to find the letters **Ff**.
Encourage them to draw a picture of
something whose name begins with **f,**
or provide old magazines from which
they can cut appropriate pictures to
glue beside the letters.

▶ You may wish to review words on the
wall chart and suggest the children
choose one of these to illustrate.
└─────────────────────────────┘

Diversity in Language and Culture

The letter **f** almost always stands for the \f\ sound (in **of,** it stands for \v\), but \f\ may be spelled in more than one way. Besides **f,** it may be spelled **ph,** as in **telephone,** and **gh,** as in **tough.** Phonetically, the sound is unlike the stop consonants \b\, \k\, and \d\ described in earlier units. Stop consonants release air suddenly. The \f\ sound, however, is a fricative, sometimes called a spirant, because air is forced through a narrow space, causing friction. In the case of the \f\ fricative, the air is forced between the upper teeth and the lower lip, so it is called a labio-dental fricative.

A related sound is \v\, which is the same as \f\ except that the vocal cords vibrate in producing \v\. (You can whisper \f\ and hold it very quietly. You can't hold \v\ in a whisper.) Children who are missing front teeth won't be able to make the \f\ sound accurately.

Some languages lack the \f\ sound. Finnish and Malay have it only in borrowed foreign words. In producing the closest Japanese sound, the teeth are not involved at all; instead, the lips are brought close together without touching, and air is blown through the opening. Sometimes such differences can affect the pronunciation of children who are learning English as a second language.

HELPING STUDENTS ACQUIRING ENGLISH

Students may need encouragement to begin to participate orally in class activities. In each unit, give greater emphasis to pronouncing spelling words, having students repeat the words, and then identifying the objects they are naming in the illustrations. You might use the following steps in sequence:

1. Students point to the object in the picture and you say the name.

2. Repeat the word aloud as the students point to the object in the picture.

3. After practice, students say the word and point to the object in the illustration.

F f

PERIOD 3

TMPRE TEMPORARY SPELLING

(p. 38)

▶ Direct the children's attention to the letter forms at the top of the page.

▶ Demonstrate the formation of capital **F** and lowercase **f**.

▶ Encourage the children to use this page in one of the following ways:

• to practice writing the letter forms;

• to draw one or more pictures of things whose names begin with the same sound as **fish** and to label each picture;

• to write words that begin with **f**.

▶ Circulate to observe the children's efforts. Ask them to tell you about their drawing and writing.

▶ Accept temporary spellings.

YOUR CHOICE:

 **SPELLING PLUS**

▶ Invite the children to practice forming **F** and **f** using finger paint. Demonstrate the activity.

◥ **ASSESS** AND **PLAN**   **p. Z19**

PERIOD 4

Getting Ready to Teach

▶ If you choose the activity under *Your Choice: Personal Writing* on this page, cut 10 to 15 fish from construction paper using the pattern on BLM 6-Fish. Write a story topic on each fish. You may wish to use some of these topics: My Family, My Pet, An Animal I Like, My Favorite Food, My Favorite TV Show, My Favorite Color, Me, What I Do at Home, My Best Friend, My Birthday.

✎ INTERACTIVE WRITING

▶ Reread "Fish" aloud.

▶ Ask the children to recall some of the facts the poem gives about fish. Write their responses in complete sentences on chart paper. Before you write a word that begins with **f**, say the word and ask the children what letter begins the word.

▶ Read the sentences aloud, pointing to each word as you read.

▶ Ask volunteers to circle the words that start with **f**.

YOUR CHOICE:

✎ PERSONAL WRITING

▶ Ask the children if they would like to fish for a story. Place the fish face-down in a "pond." (Use the floor or a table.) Allow the children to take turns choosing a fish. Read the topic on the fish and return it to the pond.

▶ Encourage the children to draw pictures of their topics. Invite them to label their pictures or write something about them.

▶ Encourage temporary spellings.

▶ Allow time for sharing.

◥ **ASSESS** AND **PLAN**   **p. Z19**

My Writing

Emergent Spelling Notes

Inventive spellers should be encouraged to label drawings using invented spelling. Leslie used semiphonetic spelling to label Humpty Dumpty. Semiphonetic spellings are often abbreviated.

Unit 6 **39**

▶ Help the children find page 39.

▶ Choose one of the *Personal Writing Activities* (A–D) listed at the bottom of this page or offer the children a choice.

▶ Accept scribblings, random letters, and invented spellings.

▶ Allow time for the children to share their pictures and writing.

ASSESS AND PLAN   p. Z19

PERSONAL WRITING ACTIVITIES

Activity A

▶ Discuss with the children different things they might see on a farm. Ask them to draw one or more farm animals.

▶ Encourage them to label their animals or write a story about them.

Activity B

▶ Ask the children to tell what they think a family is. Discuss different types of families and family members.

▶ Invite the children to draw pictures of their families.

▶ Encourage them to label the family members or to write something about the family.

Activity C

▶ Invite the children to draw funny faces and give them funny names.

▶ Encourage the children to make up a fantasy or fairy tale about their funny faces.

Activity D

▶ Ask the children to think of animals that have feathers or fur. Provide prompts if necessary.

▶ Invite the children to draw, or cut from magazines, pictures of animals that have feathers and fur.

▶ Encourage the children to label their pictures or write something about them.

ADDITIONAL LITERATURE

Bellows, Cathy. *Four Fat Rats*. Macmillan, 1987.

Ehlert, Lois. *Feathers for Lunch*. Harcourt Brace Jovanovich, 1990.

Hall, Katy, and Lisa Eisenberg. *Fishy Riddles*. Dial Books for Young Readers, 1983.

Seuss, Dr. *The Foot Book*. Random House, 1968.

Waber, Bernard. *Funny, Funny Lyle*. Houghton Mifflin, 1987.

GOALS

The children will

▶ develop phonemic awareness.

▶ identify words with the \g\ sound.

▶ associate \g\ with the letter **g**.

▶ engage in interactive writing.

▶ engage in personal writing.

▶ use invented spellings.

MATERIALS

Program materials you will need: student edition pages 40–45, *Assess and Plan File,* BLM 7-Goose

Other materials you will need: gold or yellow construction paper

Optional program materials: BLM 7-Gate

Other optional materials: glitter, glue, old magazines, scissors

PERIOD 1

Getting Ready to Teach

▶ Copy the poem from page T41 on chart paper.

▶ Cut out the goose on BLM 7-Goose and cut 10 to 15 eggs from gold or yellow construction paper, using the egg on BLM 7-Goose as a pattern.

Sharing the Poem (pp. 40–41)

▶ Help the children find pages 40 and 41.

▶ Read the poem to the class, pointing to the words as you read.

▶ Solicit personal responses to the poem. Use these responses and the illustration to guide a brief discussion of the poem.

))))))))) PHONEMIC AWARENESS

▶ Ask the children to say the word **geese** with you. Ask them what sound they hear at the beginning of **geese**. (Response: \g\) Ask if anyone has a name that begins with this sound. (Possible responses: Gordon, Gail, Gus, Gilda)

FYI Some children's names, such as George and Gina, may begin with the letter **G** but not the \g\ sound. Accept these responses, but explain the difference in sound.

▶ Read the poem again. Invite the children to raise their hands each time they hear a word that begins with the same sound as **geese**.

▶ Display the goose from BLM 7-Goose on the chalkboard. Tell the children this is Gilda the Goose and she lays golden eggs. (Read a version of *Jack and the Beanstalk* if time permits.)

▶ Explain to the children that Gilda will lay a golden egg for every word they can think of that begins with \g\. For each word they generate, display another golden egg beside the goose.

ASSESS AND **PLAN**   p. Z19

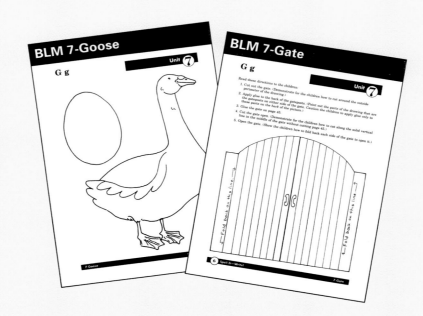

The Giggling Gaggling Gaggle of Geese

The giggling gaggling gaggle of geese,
    they keep all the cows and the chickens awake,
    they giggle all night giving nobody peace.
The giggling gaggling gaggle of geese.

The giggling gaggling gaggle of geese,
    they chased all the ducks and the swans from the lake.
Oh when will the pranks and the noise ever cease
    of the giggling gaggling gaggle of geese!

—Jack Prelutsky

40   Unit 7

Unit 7   41

The Giggling Gaggling Gaggle of Geese

The giggling gaggling gaggle of geese,
    they keep all the cows and the chickens awake,
    they giggle all night giving nobody peace.
The giggling gaggling gaggle of geese.

The giggling gaggling gaggle of geese,
    they chased all the ducks and the swans from the lake.
Oh when will the pranks and the noise ever cease
    of the giggling gaggling gaggle of geese!

—Jack Prelutsky

(The following verses do not appear in the student edition, but you may wish to share them with the children.)

The giggling gaggling gaggle of geese,
    it seems there's no end to the mischief they make,
    now they have stolen the sheep's woolen fleece.
The giggling gaggling gaggle of geese.

The giggling gaggling gaggle of geese,
    they ate all the cake that the farmer's wife baked.
The mischievous geese are now smug and obese.
The giggling gaggling gaggle of geese.

The giggling gaggling gaggle of geese,
    eating that cake was a dreadful mistake.
For when holiday comes they will make a fine feast.
The giggling gaggling gaggle of geese.

PERIOD 2

 SOUND-SYMBOL AWARENESS

(pp. 42–43)

▶ Reread "The Giggling Gaggling Gaggle of Geese" to the class.

▶ Write capital **G** and lowercase **g** on a wall chart. Identify the letter and tell the children it stands for the sound they hear at the beginning of **geese**.

▶ Ask the children to repeat after you first the sound and then the letter several times: \g\, **g**.

▶ Help the children find pages 42 and 43. Ask them if they can find a goose in the picture. Write **goose** under **Gg** on the chart. Ask them what letter begins the word **goose**. (Response: **g**)

▶ Ask the children to find other things in the picture whose names start with the same sound as **goose**.

FYI Pictured words are listed at the bottom of the reduced student page.

▶ Prompt the children as needed. At first, you may wish to control the naming of the pictured words. For example, you may ask, *"Do you see a goldfish?"* and continue in this manner for each pictured word. (Later, the children will become more aggressive in finding picture names independently.)

▶ Write each word on the chart; say the word, emphasizing the beginning sound; and ask the children to repeat it. Ask what letter begins the word.

▶ Ask the children to generate other words that begin with the same sound as **goose**. Provide prompts and wait time as needed. Add the children's responses to the wall chart.

 ASSESS AND **PLAN**   p. Z19

42   Unit 7

Pictured Words
goldfish, goat, game, gate, goose, girl, gift, guitar, gorilla, garbage truck, gold

USING THE PICTURE-SORT CARDS

After the illustrations on pages 42 and 43 have been identified and discussed, consider using the *Picture-Sort Cards* for this unit. Possible activities include the following:

▶ Duplicate the *Picture-Sort Cards* for this unit and separate them. Distribute one set of cards to individuals or small groups. Say each pictured word aloud. Ask each student to place the pointer finger of his/her right hand on a *Picture-Sort Card* and then to place the pointer finger of his/her left hand on the matching picture in the illustration in their book. (Students working in groups can take turns.) Walk around to provide assistance and praise their efforts. Encourage children to talk about the pictures.

▶ Separate the *Picture-Sort Cards* and place them in an envelope in an activity center. Label the envelope with the targeted letter, e.g., **G**. Work with individuals or small groups to match each *Picture-Sort Card* with its corresponding picture in the illustration.

For more information on using *Picture-Sort Cards,* see the *Picture-Sort Card Book.*

YOUR CHOICE:

SPELLING PLUS

▶ Help the children find page 162.

▶ Ask them to find the letters **Gg**. Encourage them to draw a picture of something whose name begins with **g** as in **goose,** or provide old magazines from which they can cut appropriate pictures to glue beside the letters.

▶ You may wish to review words on the wall chart and suggest the children choose one of these to illustrate.

YOUR CHOICE:

SPELLING PLUS

▶ Review with the children the words on the wall chart that begin with **g**. Ask the children to help you write a silly sentence using words that begin with **g**. Provide prompts or offer one or two examples to stimulate the children's thinking. Examples: The good gorilla gave the gold to the goose. Gary got a gallon of green golf goggles at a gallery.

▶ Write the children's suggestions on the chalkboard or a wall chart.

▶ Read all the sentences, pointing to the words as you say them. Encourage the children to repeat the sentences with you.

▶ Invite the children to copy a sentence of their choice and illustrate it. Compile the illustrations and sentences in a class book.

Diversity in Language and Culture

The letter **g** stands for two sounds in English. They are usually referred to as "hard" **g** (as in **gold**) and "soft" **g** (as in **gem**). Despite the shared spelling, these sounds are quite different from each other.

This unit focuses on the "hard" **g** sound, **g**\\. Phonetically, **g**\\ is a stop consonant sound, closely related to **k**\\. The air is completely blocked by the back of the tongue against the roof of the mouth at the soft palate, or velum. While \\k\\ is a voiceless velar stop, \\g\\ is a voiced velar stop: the vocal cords start vibrating as air is released.

The \\g\\ sound appears in most languages and is produced early by babies (as in **gaga**). Some languages, however, including Arabic and Thai, don't have \\g\\.

HELPING STUDENTS ACQUIRING ENGLISH

Help students overcome their reluctance to take part verbally in class by beginning their participation with activities that may be more comfortable for them. This might take one of these forms:

• drawing;

• some type of physical action, such as pointing to objects in illustrations;

• doing actions you ask them to do.

For this unit, you might use instruction words that begin with **g**\\ such as "Give...," "Go...," "Get...," etc.

Letters and Words

Gg

TMPRE **TEMPORARY SPELLING**

(p. 44)

▶ Direct the children's attention to the letter forms at the top of the page.

▶ Demonstrate the formation of capital **G** and lowercase **g**.

▶ Encourage the children to use this page in one of the following ways:

- to practice writing the letter forms;

- to draw one or more pictures of things whose names begin with the same sound as **goose** and to label each picture;

- to write words that begin with **g** as in **goose**.

▶ Circulate to observe the children's efforts. Ask them to tell you about their drawing and writing.

▶ Accept temporary spellings.

YOUR CHOICE:

 SPELLING PLUS

▶ Invite the children to practice forming **G** and **g** using glitter and glue. Demonstrate the activity.

ASSESS AND **PLAN**   p. Z19

PERIOD 4

 INTERACTIVE WRITING

▶ Reread "The Giggling Gaggling Gaggle of Geese" aloud.

▶ Ask the children to think of a sentence about something the geese did in the poem.

▶ Write their responses on chart paper. Before you write a word beginning with **g,** ask the children to tell you what letter it starts with.

▶ Encourage the children to think of other things geese do besides make noise. Add these responses to the chart in sentence form.

▶ Read the sentences aloud, pointing to each word as you read.

▶ Ask volunteers to circle the words that start with **g**.

YOUR CHOICE:

 PERSONAL WRITING

▶ Ask several volunteers to demonstrate giggling. Then ask the whole class to giggle together.

▶ Invite the children to draw a picture of something that makes them giggle. Encourage them to label their pictures or write a sentence about them.

▶ Encourage temporary spellings.

▶ Allow time for sharing.

ASSESS AND **PLAN**   p. Z19

My Writing

Emergent Spelling Notes

Leslie used phonetic spelling to label Huggable Cat. All the sounds in the words are represented in phonetic spellings.

HEP-EBL-CAT

PERSONAL WRITING   p. 45

▶ Help the children find page 45.

▶ Choose one of the *Personal Writing Activities* (A–D) listed at the bottom of this page or offer the children a choice.

▶ Accept scribblings, random letters, and invented spellings.

▶ Allow time for the children to share their pictures and writing.

ASSESS AND PLAN   p. Z19

PERSONAL WRITING ACTIVITIES

Activity A

▶ Discuss with the children gifts that do not cost money.

▶ Invite them to draw a picture showing a gift they could give that would not cost money.

▶ Encourage them to write a sentence describing the gift.

Activity B

▶ Distribute BLM 7-Gate. Read the directions to the children and guide them as they carry out each step.

▶ Ask them to open their gates and draw a picture of something that might be behind the gate. Then tell them to close the gate and write a few words describing what is behind the gate.

Activity C

▶ Ask the children to write **GO** at the top of the page. Ask them to name things that go. (Possible responses: cars, trucks, planes, people, merry-go-rounds, birds, Superman)

▶ Invite the children to draw a picture of something that goes and to label it or write something about it.

Activity D

▶ Ask the children to imagine they are looking for gold treasure. Suggest that this treasure might be sunk at the bottom of the sea, buried in a hole, or waiting at the end of a rainbow.

▶ Ask the children to draw a picture of the treasure they are looking for and to write a story about how the treasure got there.

ADDITIONAL LITERATURE

Brown, Margaret Wise. *Goodnight Moon.* Harper & Row, 1947.

De Regniers, Beatrice Schenk. *Jack and the Beanstalk.* Atheneum, 1985.

Saunders, Susan. *The Golden Goose.* Scholastic/Hardcover Books, 1988.

Spier, Peter. *Gobble, Growl, Grunt.* Doubleday, 1971.

Wildsmith, Brian. *Give a Dog a Bone.* Pantheon Books, 1985.

G O A L S

The children will

▶ develop phonemic awareness.

▶ identify words with the \h\ sound.

▶ associate \h\ with the letter **h**.

▶ engage in interactive writing.

▶ engage in personal writing.

▶ use invented spellings.

M A T E R I A L S

Program materials you will need: student edition pages 46–51, *Assess and Plan File*

Optional program materials: BLMs 8-Ha! Ha! Ha! and 8-Heart

Other optional materials: old magazines, scissors, glue, crayons

P E R I O D 1

Getting Ready to Teach

▶ Copy the poem from page T47 on chart paper.

Sharing the Poem (pp. 46–47)

▶ Help the children find pages 46 and 47.

▶ Read the poem to the class, pointing to the words as you read.

▶ Solicit personal responses to the poem. Use these responses and the illustration to guide a brief discussion of the poem.

))))))))) PHONEMIC AWARENESS

▶ Ask the children to say the word **house** with you. Ask them what sound they hear at the beginning of **house**. (Response: \h\) Ask if anyone has a name that begins with this sound. (Possible responses: Harry, Hope, Howard, Heather)

▶ Read the poem again. Invite the children to raise their hands each time they hear a word that begins with the same sound as **house**.

▶ Ask the children to recall the words in the poem that begin like **house** and that name a kind of house. (Responses: **hill, hive, hole**)

▶ Encourage the children to look around the classroom for objects whose names begin like **house**. (Possible responses: hair, hands, hats)

▶ Tell the children you will ask them several riddles. Explain that the answer to each riddle is a word that begins with the same sound as **house**. Use these riddles:

- What has five fingers? (**hand**)

- What animal can you ride? (**horse**)

- What word means the opposite of sad? (**happy**)

- What is a house for your brain? (**head**)

- What word means the opposite of easy? (**hard**)

◢ **ASSESS** AND **PLAN**　　　p. Z19

**A House Is
a House for Me**

A hill is a house for an ant, an ant.
A hive is a house for a bee.
A hole is house for a mole or a mouse
And a house is a house for me!

—Mary Ann Hoberman

A House Is
a House for Me

A hill is a house for an ant, an ant.
A hive is a house for a bee.
A hole is house for a mole or a mouse
And a house is a house for me!

—Mary Ann Hoberman

*(The following verses do not appear in the
student edition, but you may wish to share
them with the children.)*

A garage is a house for a car or a truck.
A hangar's a house for a plane.
A dock or a slip is a house for a ship
And a terminal's house for a train.

The cooky jar's home to the cookies.
The breadbox is home to the bread.
My coat is a house for my body.
My hat is a house for my head.

A glove is a house for a hand, a hand.
A stocking's a house for a knee.
A shoe or a boot is a house for a foot
And a house is a house for me!

)) **SOUND-SYMBOL AWARENESS**

(pp. 48–49)

▶ Reread "A House Is a House for Me" to the class.

▶ Write capital **H** and lowercase **h** on a wall chart. Identify the letter and tell the children it stands for the sound they hear at the beginning of **house**.

▶ Ask the children to repeat after you first the sound and then the letter several times: \h\, **h**.

▶ Help the children find pages 48 and 49. Ask them if they can find a house in the picture. Write **house** under **Hh** on the chart. Ask them what letter begins the word **house**. (Response: **h**)

▶ Ask the children to find other things in the picture whose names start with the same sound as **house**.

FYI Pictured words are listed at the bottom of the reduced student page.

▶ Prompt the children as needed. At first, you may wish to control the naming of the pictured words. For example, you may ask, *"Do you see a hen?"* and continue in this manner for each pictured word. (Later, the children will become more aggressive in finding picture names independently.)

▶ Write each word on the chart; say the word, emphasizing the beginning sound; and ask the children to repeat it. Ask what letter begins the word.

▶ Ask the children to generate other words that begin with the same sound as **house**. Provide prompts and wait time as needed. Add the children's responses to the wall chart.

Pictured Words

house, hen, helicopter, horn, horse, heart, hippopotamus, hammer, hat, harmonica, hamburger

 ASSESS AND **PLAN**   p. Z19

USING THE PICTURE-SORT CARDS

After the illustrations on pages 48 and 49 have been identified and discussed, consider using the *Picture-Sort Cards* for this unit. Possible activities include the following:

▶ Duplicate the *Picture-Sort Cards* for this unit and separate them. Distribute one set of cards to individuals or small groups. Say each pictured word aloud. Ask each student to place the pointer finger of his/her right hand on a *Picture-Sort Card* and then to place the pointer finger of his/her left hand on the matching picture in the illustration in their book. (Students working in

groups can take turns.) Walk around to provide assistance and praise their efforts. Encourage children to talk about the pictures.

▶ Separate the *Picture-Sort Cards* and place them in an envelope in an activity center. Label the envelope with the targeted letter, e.g., **H**. Work with individuals or small groups to match each *Picture-Sort Card* with its corresponding picture in the illustration.

For more information on using *Picture-Sort Cards,* see the *Picture-Sort Card Book.*

Unit 8 **49**

YOUR CHOICE:

 SPELLING PLUS

▶ Help the children find page 162.

▶ Ask them to find the letters **Hh**. Encourage them to draw a picture of something whose name begins with **h**, or provide old magazines from which they can cut appropriate pictures to glue beside the letters.

▶ You may wish to review words on the wall chart and suggest the children choose one of these to illustrate.

Diversity in Language and Culture

The letter **h** is a very useful one in English. In addition to representing the breathy \h\ sound in such words as **house** and **hill**, it is a "helper" letter in representing more complex sounds, such as **ch** in **church** and **th** in **thin**, and is often silent (**honest, straight**). Some speakers also use \h\ in pronouncing **wh** in such words as **which** and **when**.

This unit focuses on the \h\ sound. Linguists have various ways of explaining the production of this sound. The simplest way is as a puff of air or a voiceless breath. The letter **h** shows up in most Western European languages, but in French and Spanish, it is always silent. French **homme** and Spanish **hombre,** both of which mean "man," are pronounced \uhm\ and \ohm-bray\. In each word, the **h** is silent. Other languages that lack the \h\ sound include Portuguese, Italian, and Russian.

Children from these language backgrounds who are learning English as a second language may be inclined to omit \h\ when speaking English, or they may substitute another sound.

HELPING STUDENTS ACQUIRING ENGLISH

As mentioned in *Diversity in Language and Culture* in this unit, the letter **h** is silent in some languages. Help students overcome a tendency to leave out the **h** when pronouncing English words by telling them that **h** is often pronounced in English. Explain that **h** is the "laughing letter." On the chalkboard, write **Ho! Ha! He!** Then, as you point to each word, laugh with that vowel sound, "Ho, ho, ho," etc., imitating true laughter. Then ask the children to do the same as you point to each word. Finally, together with the students, do a long laugh using each of the vowel sounds several times.

PERIOD 3

 **TEMPORARY SPELLING**

(p. 50)

▶ Direct the children's attention to the letter forms at the top of the page.

▶ Demonstrate the formation of capital **H** and lowercase **h**.

▶ Encourage the children to use this page in one of the following ways:

- to practice writing the letter forms;
- to draw one or more pictures of things whose names begin with the same sound as **house** and to label each picture;
- to write words that begin with **h**.

▶ Circulate to observe the children's efforts. Ask them to tell you about their drawing and writing.

▶ Accept temporary spellings.

YOUR CHOICE:

 SPELLING PLUS

▶ Invite the children to practice forming **H** and **h** using tactile media of their choice, such as building blocks or bricks, clay, glitter, straws, or string.

◤ **ASSESS** AND **PLAN**　　p. Z19

 **Letters and Words**

Hh

PERIOD 4

✏ **INTERACTIVE WRITING**

▶ Reread "A House Is a House for Me" aloud.

▶ Write on the chalkboard or on chart paper *Things You Need to Build a House.* Read the title, pointing to each word. Encourage the children to name tools and materials needed to build a house. List their responses. Ask the children to find words in the list that begin with **h**.

YOUR CHOICE:

✏ **PERSONAL WRITING**

▶ Invite the children to draw a picture of a house. Encourage them to think not only of houses for people but also of other kinds of houses, such as houses for animals (nest, aquarium, cage) and things (refrigerator, bookcase, drawer, closet). You might also suggest they think of storybook houses (the candy house in *Hansel and Gretel,* the shoe in "The Old Woman Who Lived in a Shoe").

▶ Ask the children to write a few words describing the house and who lives in it.

▶ Encourage temporary spellings.

▶ Allow time for sharing.

 ASSESS AND **PLAN**　　p. Z19

My Writing

Emergent Spelling Notes

Like many children, Leslie experiences five stages of spelling development. Here is a sample of her spelling at the precommunicative stage.

Leslie's Spelling

EOiiVEliOE
NEMliEDN
MDRMNE

Translation

(Story describing a picture of a flock of butterflies)

Unit 8 **51**

PERIOD 5

PERSONAL WRITING p. 51

▶ Help the children find page 51.

▶ Choose one of the *Personal Writing Activities* (A–D) listed at the bottom of this page or offer the children a choice.

▶ Accept scribblings, random letters, and invented spellings.

▶ Allow time for the children to share their pictures and writing.

YOUR CHOICE: Review

▶ Use the third and fourth pages of Units 1–7 to review sound-letter relationships. Encourage the children to find the items in each picture whose names begin with the letter shown at the top of the left-hand page.

▶ Pronounce words beginning with the sound-letter relationships you wish to review. Ask the children to pronounce the initial sound in each word or to name the letter that stands for that sound. Use these words: **dive, boot, foot, body, coat, ever, gorilla, hello, ask, copy, dance, fun, good, help**.

ASSESS AND **PLAN** p. Z19

PERSONAL WRITING ACTIVITIES

Activity A

▶ Distribute BLM 8-Ha! Ha! Ha! Read the words and ask the children to repeat them with you several times.

▶ Ask the children to color the letters, cut along the dashed line, and glue the words on page 51.

▶ Invite the children to draw a picture of something that makes them laugh. Encourage them to write something about the picture.

Activity B

▶ Ask the children to place one hand, palm down, with fingers spread, on page 51 and to draw around it with a crayon.

▶ Ask them to write on each finger a word or phrase that tells something they do with their hands, or ask them to write on each finger a word that begins with **h**.

Activity C

▶ Ask the children to draw a picture of the place they live.

▶ Encourage them to write something about it.

Activity D

▶ Distribute BLM 8-Heart. Ask the children to cut it out and decorate it like a valentine.

▶ Encourage them to write on the heart the name of the person to whom they would like to give the valentine.

▶ Ask them to write on page 51 their reasons for giving a valentine to this person.

ADDITIONAL LITERATURE

Bohdal, Susi. *Harry the Hare*. North-South Books, 1986.

Carle, Eric. *A House for Hermit Crab*. Picture Book Studio, 1987.

Hadithi, Mwenye. *Hot Hippo*. Little, Brown, 1986.

Martin, Bill, Jr., and John Archambault. *Here Are My Hands*. Henry Holt, 1985.

Slepian, Jan, and Ann Seidler. *The Hungry Thing*. Follett, 1967.

G O A L S

The children will

▶ develop phonemic awareness.

▶ identify words with the **short i** sound.

▶ associate the **short i** sound with the letter **i**.

▶ engage in interactive writing.

▶ engage in personal writing.

▶ use invented spellings.

M A T E R I A L S

Program materials you will need: student edition pages 52–57, *Assess and Plan File*

Other materials you will need: pencils or sticks

Optional materials: old magazines, scissors, glue, ballpoint pens or ink and ink brushes

P E R I O D 1

Getting Ready to Teach

▶ Copy the poem from page T53 on chart paper.

Sharing the Poem (pp. 52–53)

▶ Help the children find pages 52 and 53.

▶ Read the poem to the class, pointing to the words as you read.

▶ Solicit personal responses to the poem. Use these responses and the illustration to guide a brief discussion of the poem.

PHONEMIC AWARENESS

▶ Ask the children to say the word **inch** with you. Ask them what sound they hear at the beginning of **inch**. (Response: \i\) Ask if anyone has a name that begins with this sound. (Possible responses: Imogene, Isabel, Ignatius, Israel)

FYI Some children's names, such as Ira, Ivy, and Inez, may begin with the letter **I** but not the **short i** sound. Accept these responses, but explain the difference in sound.

▶ Distribute pencils or sticks. Read the poem again. Invite the children to beat out the rhythm with their pencils or sticks as you read.

▶ Tell the children you will say a word in "slow motion" and ask them to say it in a normal way. For example, if you say **pick** as \p\-\i\-\k\, the children should respond "pick." Each time they say a word correctly, draw a stick on the chalkboard. Challenge them to build a big pile of sticks.

▶ Use words that have a **short i** sound and only two or three phonemes, such as **if, in, is, big, did, miss, pig, sit, hill, Jim, fit, Jill, win, dig, kick**.

◢ **ASSESS** AND **PLAN**   p. Z19

The Pickety Fence

The pickety fence
The pickety fence
Give it a lick it's
The pickety fence
Give it a lick it's
A clickety fence
Give it a lick it's
A lickety fence
Give it a lick
Give it a lick
Give it a lick
With a rickety stick
Pickety
Pickety
Pickety
Pick

—David McCord

The Pickety Fence

The pickety fence
The pickety fence
Give it a lick it's
The pickety fence
Give it a lick it's
A clickety fence
Give it a lick it's
A lickety fence
Give it a lick
Give it a lick
Give it a lick
With a rickety stick
Pickety
Pickety
Pickety
Pick

—David McCord

54 · Unit 9

PERIOD 2

 SOUND-SYMBOL AWARENESS

(pp. 54–55)

▶ Reread "The Pickety Fence" to the class.

▶ Write capital **I** and lowercase **i** on a wall chart. Identify the letter and tell the children it stands for the sound they hear at the beginning of **inch**.

▶ Ask the children to repeat after you first the sound and then the letter several times: \i\, **i**.

▶ Help the children find pages 54 and 55. Ask them if they can find an inch in the picture. Write **inch** under **Ii** on the chart. Ask them what letter begins the word **inch**. (Response: **i**)

▶ Ask the children to find other things in the picture whose names start with the same sound as **inch**.

FYI ▷ Pictured words are listed at the bottom of the reduced student page.

▶ Prompt the children as needed. At first, you may wish to control the naming of the pictured words. For example, you may ask, *"Do you see an igloo?"* and continue in this manner for each pictured word. (Later, the children will become more aggressive in finding picture names independently.)

▶ Write each word on the chart; say the word, emphasizing the **short i** sound; and ask the children to repeat it. Ask what letter begins the word.

▶ Ask the children to generate other words that begin with the same sound as **inch**. Provide prompts and wait time as needed. Add the children's responses to the wall chart.

Pictured Words
short i: iguana, igloo, insect, inch, ink
long i: ice, ice skates, icicle, iron, ivy

YOUR CHOICE:

 SPELLING PLUS

▶ If you wish to introduce **long i,** write **ice** on a wall chart. Say the word and ask the children to repeat it. Ask them what sound they hear at the beginning of **ice**. (Response: The children should say the **long i** sound, pronounced as in **eye**.) Ask what letter begins the word **ice**. (Response: **i**)

▶ Ask the children if they can find anything in the picture on pages 54 and 55 whose name begins with the same sound as **ice**. Elicit responses as you did for words beginning with the **short i** sound.

▶ Write each word on the chart; say the word, emphasizing the **long i** sound; and ask the children to repeat it.

▶ Ask the children to generate other words that begin with the same sound as **ice**. Provide prompts and wait time as needed. Add responses to the wall chart.

▲ **ASSESS** AND **PLAN**   p. Z19

USING THE PICTURE-SORT CARDS

After the illustrations on pages 54 and 55 have been identified and discussed, consider using the *Picture-Sort Cards* for this unit. For more information on using *Picture-Sort Cards,* see page T48 or the *Picture-Sort Card Book.*

Unit 9 **55**

Diversity in Language and Culture

This unit focuses on the basic **short i** and **long i** sounds.

Vowel sounds can be described by the position of the tongue (front or back) and the jaw (high or low), as well as the tenseness of the tongue muscle. The \i\ in **pickety** is a high front lax vowel, which means the tongue is pushed forward in the mouth, the jaw is relatively closed, and the muscle is somewhat relaxed. The closest relative to this sound is the vowel sound in such words as **meet** and **Pete,** which is also a high front vowel, but is pronounced with the tongue muscle tensed. (Say **hit** and **heat** alternately. The tongue is a little higher in **heat,** but also more tense.)

The **long i** sound in **kite** is a diphthong—a vowel sound that glides into a second vowel sound within the same syllable, in this case a low vowel followed by a high vowel. If you exaggerate the pronunciation, you can feel your jaw change position from the first part of the diphthong to the end.

Not all languages have these sounds. Spanish, for instance, does not have the separate vowel sounds of **heat** and **hit.** For this reason, Spanish speakers often confuse such English words. (Some might pronounce **it** as **eat,** for instance.)

Many languages lack the sounds of English diphthongs, and learners may need special practice in pronouncing words with the **long i** sound.

HELPING STUDENTS ACQUIRING ENGLISH

The **short i** sound of English may not be familiar to students with certain primary languages. The \i\ sound of the **short i** does not exist in Spanish, for example, and the **long i** of English is produced with a diphthong (\ai\ or \ay\). Examples of words with this sound include **baile** (**dance**) and **mayo** (**May**). Pronounce the **short i** several times with students, then add consonants (e.g., **pip, zip, lip**), repeating each word several times until students pronounce the words correctly.

T55

I i

PERIOD 3

 **TEMPORARY SPELLING**

(p. 56)

▶ Direct the children's attention to the letter forms at the top of the page.

▶ Demonstrate the formation of capital **I** and lowercase **i**.

▶ Encourage the children to use this page in one of the following ways:

• to practice writing the letter forms;

• to draw one or more pictures of things whose names begin with the same sound as **inch** and to label each picture;

• to write words that begin with **i**.

▶ Circulate to observe the children's efforts. Ask them to tell you about their drawing and writing.

▶ Accept temporary spellings.

┌─────────────────────────────────┐
YOUR CHOICE:

 SPELLING PLUS

▶ Invite the children to practice forming **I** and **i** using ink. Demonstrate the activity.
└─────────────────────────────────┘

ASSESS AND **PLAN**   p. Z19

PERIOD 4

 **INTERACTIVE WRITING**

▶ Reread "The Pickety Fence" aloud.

▶ Tell the children the fence in the poem and in the picture on pages 52 and 53 is called a picket fence. Ask them to describe other kinds of fences they have seen. If they have trouble describing the fences in words, invite them to draw pictures on the chalkboard.

▶ Ask the children what the fence in the poem was used for. (Possible response: to make noise or music) Ask them to describe other uses for fences. (Possible responses: to keep someone or something outside a space, to keep someone or something inside a space, to provide something for flowers or vines to climb)

▶ Write all the children's responses on chart paper in sentence form.

┌─────────────────────────────────┐
YOUR CHOICE:

PERSONAL WRITING

▶ Ask the children to draw a picture of a fence and to write what the fence is used for. Ask them to circle any words in their writing that begin with **i**.

▶ Encourage temporary spellings.

▶ Allow time for sharing.
└─────────────────────────────────┘

ASSESS AND **PLAN**   p. Z19

My Writing

Emergent Spelling Notes

Like many children, Leslie experiences five stages of spelling development. Here is a sample of her spelling at the semiphonetic stage.

Leslie's Spelling	Conventional Spelling
ALD	allowed
GIZ	girls
HMT DPD	Humpty Dumpty

PERSONAL WRITING   p. 57

▶ Help the children find page 57.

▶ Choose one of the *Personal Writing Activities* (A–D) listed at the bottom of this page or offer the children a choice.

▶ Activities A and B focus on words with **short i** sounds. Activities C and D may be used if you have introduced **long i**.

▶ Accept scribblings, random letters, and invented spellings.

▶ Allow time for the children to share their pictures and writing.

ASSESS AND PLAN   p. Z19

PERSONAL WRITING ACTIVITIES

Activity A

▶ Ask the children to write the word **If** at the top of page 57.

▶ Invite them to write a sentence beginning with **If** and illustrate it.

Activity B

▶ Invite the children to draw or cut from magazines pictures of insects.

▶ Encourage them to label their insects and write a fact or opinion about insects.

Activity C

▶ Write *Who Am I?* on the chalkboard. Ask the children to write this title at the top of page 57.

▶ Invite the children to write about themselves. Suggest they illustrate their accounts or ideas with pictures of themselves or things they're interested in.

Activity D

▶ Invite the children to draw a picture of their favorite ice-cream dish and to write a description telling how to make it.

ADDITIONAL LITERATURE

Maris, Ron. *I Wish I Could Fly.* Greenwillow Books, 1986.

Morimoto, Junko, illustrator. *The Inch Boy.* Viking Kestrel, 1986.

Silverstein, Shel. "Ickle Me, Pickle Me, Tickle Me Too," in *Where the Sidewalk Ends.* Harper & Row, 1974.

Yue, Charlotte, and David Yue. *The Igloo.* Houghton Mifflin, 1988. (This book is for older children but could be used to share pictures and discuss the Inuits' way of life.)

GOALS

The children will

▶ develop phonemic awareness.

▶ identify words with the \j\ sound.

▶ associate \j\ with the letter **j**.

▶ engage in interactive writing.

▶ engage in personal writing.

▶ use invented spellings.

MATERIALS

Program materials you will need: student edition pages 58–63, *Assess and Plan File,* BLM 10-Jack and Jill

Optional program materials: BLM 10-Safety

Other optional materials: *The Corner Grocery Store* by Raffi (audiocassette), audiocassette player, rhythm instruments, old magazines, scissors, glue, jelly beans, crayons

PERIOD 1

Getting Ready to Teach

▶ Copy the poem from page T59 on chart paper.

▶ Cut the Jack and Jill figures from BLM 10-Jack and Jill. Color them if you wish.

Sharing the Poem (pp. 58–59)

▶ Help the children find pages 58 and 59.

▶ Read the poem to the class, pointing to the words as you read.

▶ Solicit personal responses to the poem. Use these responses and the illustration to guide a brief discussion of the poem.

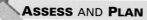 **PHONEMIC AWARENESS**

▶ Ask the children to say the word **Jack** with you. Ask them what sound they hear at the beginning of **Jack**. (Response: \j\) Ask if anyone has a name that begins with this sound. (Possible responses: Judy, Joyce, John, Jeff, Geraldine, George)

▶ Read the poem again. Invite the children to raise their hands each time they hear a word that begins with the same sound as **Jack**.

▶ Encourage the children to look around the classroom for objects whose names begin like **Jack**. (Possible responses: jackets, jars, jeans, jewelry)

▶ Draw a hill on the chalkboard and position the Jack and Jill figures at the bottom. Tell the children they can help Jack and Jill get safely up and down the hill by making new words. Invite them to add \j\ at the beginning of words you say. Use these words: **am** (**jam**), **are** (**jar**), **aw** (**jaw**), **oak** (**joke**), **ugh** (**jug**), **ump** (**jump**). As the children respond, move Jack and Jill up the hill and down the other side.

ASSESS AND **PLAN**   p. Z19

Jack and Jill

Jack and Jill went up the hill,
    To fetch a pail of water;
Jack fell down, and broke his crown,
    And Jill came tumbling after.

Then up Jack got and off did trot,
    As fast as he could caper,
To old Dame Dob, who patched his nob
    With vinegar and brown paper.

))) **SOUND-SYMBOL AWARENESS**

(pp. 60–61)

▶ Reread "Jack and Jill" to the class.

▶ Write capital **J** and lowercase **j** on a wall chart. Identify the letter and tell the children it stands for the sound they hear at the beginning of **Jack**.

▶ Ask the children to repeat after you first the sound and then the letter several times: \j\, **j**.

▶ Help the children find pages 60 and 61. Ask them if they can find a jacket in the picture. Write **jacket** under **Jj** on the chart. Ask them what letter begins the word **jacket**. (Response: **j**)

▶ Ask the children to find other things in the picture whose names start with the same sound as **Jack**.

FYI Pictured words are listed at the bottom of the reduced student page.

▶ Prompt the children as needed. At first, you may wish to control the naming of the pictured words. For example, you may ask, *"Do you see a jet?"* and continue in this manner for each pictured word. (Later, the children will become more aggressive in finding picture names independently.)

▶ Write each word on the chart; say the word, emphasizing the beginning sound; and ask the children to repeat it. Ask what letter begins the word.

▶ Ask the children to generate other words that begin with the same sound as **Jack**. Provide prompts and wait time as needed. Add the children's responses to the wall chart.

FYI If children state words that begin with **g**, write these words on the wall chart in a separate column and explain that sometimes the \j\ sound is spelled **g**.

Pictured Words
jet, jacket, jeans, jeep, jam or **jelly, jewelry, juice, jack-in-the-box, juggle, jar**

▶ **ASSESS** AND **PLAN** p. Z19

USING THE PICTURE-SORT CARDS

After the illustrations on pages 60 and 61 have been identified and discussed, consider using the *Picture-Sort Cards* for this unit. Possible activities include the following:

▶ Duplicate the *Picture-Sort Cards* for this unit and separate them. Distribute one set of cards to individuals or small groups. Say each pictured word aloud. Ask each student to place the pointer finger of his/her right hand on a *Picture-Sort Card* and then to place the pointer finger of his/her left hand on the matching picture in the illustration in their book. (Students working in groups can take turns.) Walk around to provide assistance and praise their efforts. Encourage children to talk about the pictures.

▶ Separate the *Picture-Sort Cards* and place them in an envelope in an activity center. Label the envelope with the targeted letter, e.g., **J**. Work with individuals or small groups to match each *Picture-Sort Card* with its corresponding picture in the illustration.

For more information on using *Picture-Sort Cards*, see the *Picture-Sort Card Book*.

YOUR CHOICE:

SPELLING PLUS

▶ Ask the children to listen as you play "Jig Along Home" from the audiocassette *The Corner Grocery Store* by Raffi.

▶ Ask the children to move to the music as you play the song again.

▶ Provide rhythm instruments for the children to play along with the song.

Unit 10 **61**

Diversity in Language and Culture

The letter **j** stands for a relatively complicated sound: \j\ as in **jungle**. In producing this sound, some phonetic gymnastics occur. At the beginning of the sound, the mouth actually produces \d\ and follows it immediately with \zh\ (as in **pleasure**).

Many languages do not have this sound, called an "affricate." It is a combination of \d\, which stops air flow, followed by the \zh\ fricative, which creates a hissing sound. French has the \zh\ sound, but \j\ shows up only in a few borrowed words, such as **jazz**.

Young learners frequently have

problems making this complicated sound. Since it can be broken down into \d\ and \zh\, it sometimes helps to ask learners to make the two sounds separately and then try to put them together.

The closest related sound to \j\ is \ch\, as in **chin**. The \ch\ sound is identical to \j\ in its production, but \ch\ is unvoiced (the vocal cords are not vibrating), whereas \j\ is voiced (the vocal cords are vibrating). Standard Spanish has \ch\ but not \j\.

HELPING STUDENTS ACQUIRING ENGLISH

Have students work with a study buddy to acquire the sound of **j** in English. (Study buddies may be students whose primary language is English or students who have acquired a more advanced level of English.) Spanish-speaking students may tend to pronounce the letter **j** as \h\ if they have some knowledge of the alphabet in Spanish. Ask the students and study buddies to say the words pictured in the illustration on pages 60 and 61 several times, pointing to each object and repeating its name aloud. Emphasize the *Your Choice: Spelling Plus* activity on page T60 with students.

PERIOD 3

 **TEMPORARY SPELLING**

(p. 62)

▶ Direct the children's attention to the letter forms at the top of the page.

▶ Demonstrate the formation of capital **J** and lowercase **j**.

▶ Encourage the children to use this page in one of the following ways:

- to practice writing the letter forms;

- to draw one or more pictures of things whose names begin with the same sound as **Jack** and to label each picture;

- to write words that begin with **j**.

▶ Circulate to observe the children's efforts. Ask them to tell you about their drawing and writing.

▶ Accept temporary spellings.

YOUR CHOICE:

 SPELLING PLUS

▶ Invite the children to practice forming **J** and **j** using jelly beans. Demonstrate the activity.

 **ASSESS** AND **PLAN**   **p. Z19**

Letters and Words

J j

PERIOD 4

INTERACTIVE WRITING

▶ Reread "Jack and Jill" aloud. Let the children recite the parts they know by heart.

▶ Ask the children to recall something that happened in the poem. Write their responses on chart paper.

▶ Before you write a word that begins with a sound-letter relationship that has been previously introduced (**a** through **j**), you may wish to say the word and ask the children to name the letter that spells the beginning sound. For example, if someone offers the sentence "Jack fell down," you can ask the class to spell the beginning letter in **Jack, fell,** and **down**. (Use your judgment to decide whether this activity is appropriate for your class at this time.)

YOUR CHOICE:

PERSONAL WRITING

▶ Discuss Jack and Jill's accident briefly. Discuss safety practices and ways to avoid accidents.

▶ Distribute BLM 10-Safety. Discuss the pictures.

▶ Invite the children to color and cut out one of the pictures, glue it on a sheet of paper, and write something to describe the pictured safety precaution.

▶ Encourage temporary spellings.

▶ Allow time for sharing.

ASSESS AND **PLAN**   **p. Z19**

My Writing

Emergent Spelling Notes

Like many children, Leslie experiences five stages of spelling development. Here is a sample of her spelling at the phonetic stage.

Leslie's Spelling

TAS AS E PACHRR FER MOM

I HEP UOU LEK TAS PACHERR EV DNL DEK AND DASY DEC.

Conventional Spelling

This is a picture for Mom.

I hope you like this picture of Donald Duck and Daisy Duck.

Unit 10 **63**

PERIOD 5

PERSONAL WRITING p. 63

- ▶ Help the children find page 63.
- ▶ Choose one of the *Personal Writing Activities* (A–D) listed at the bottom of this page or offer the children a choice.
- ▶ Accept scribblings, random letters, and invented spellings.
- ▶ Allow time for the children to share their pictures and writing.

YOUR CHOICE:

 SPELLING PLUS

- ▶ Invite a juggler to perform for your class.
- ▶ Encourage the class to help you write a thank-you note after the juggler's visit.

ASSESS AND **PLAN** p. Z19

PERSONAL WRITING ACTIVITIES

Activity A

- ▶ Discuss get-well cards with the class.
- ▶ Invite the children to compose a get-well card for Jack or for someone else they know who is ill.

Activity B

- ▶ Invite the children to draw a picture of the fruits or vegetables their favorite juice is made of.
- ▶ Encourage the children to label their pictures or write something about them.

Activity C

- ▶ Invite the children to tell you about jobs they do at home. Make a list of these on the chalkboard or on chart paper.

- ▶ Ask the children to write a sentence about a job they do at home. Encourage them to illustrate their writing.

Activity D

- ▶ Talk to the class about jungle environments and the animals that live in them.
- ▶ Invite the children to draw a picture of an animal that lives in the jungle.
- ▶ Encourage them to label the picture or write a jungle story.

ADDITIONAL LITERATURE

Fleischman, Paul. *Joyful Noise: Poems for Two Voices.* Harper & Row/Charlotte Zolotow Books, 1988.

Hawkins, Colin. *Flip the Page Rhyming Books: Jen the Hen.* Putnam Publishing Group, 1985.

Kalan, Robert. *Jump, Frog, Jump!* Greenwillow Books, 1981.

Neitzel, Shirley. *The Jacket I Wear in the Snow.* Greenwillow Books, 1989.

GOALS

The children will

▶ develop phonemic awareness.

▶ identify words with the \k\ sound.

▶ associate \k\ with the letter **k**.

▶ engage in interactive writing.

▶ engage in personal writing.

▶ use invented spellings.

MATERIALS

Program materials you will need: student edition pages 64–69, *Assess and Plan File*, BLM 11-Mitten

Other materials you will need: construction paper or wallpaper samples

Optional materials: old magazines, scissors, glue, popping corn

PERIOD 1

Getting Ready to Teach

▶ Copy the poem from page T65 on chart paper.

Sharing the Poem (pp. 64–65)

▶ Help the children find pages 64 and 65.

▶ Read the poem to the class, pointing to the words as you read.

▶ Solicit personal responses to the poem. Use these responses and the illustration to guide a brief discussion of the poem.

PHONEMIC AWARENESS

▶ Ask the children to say the word **kitten** with you. Ask them what sound they hear at the beginning of **kitten**. (Response: \k\) Ask if anyone has a name that begins with this sound. (Possible responses: Kate, Kevin, Keith, Karen, Carol, Calvin)

▶ Read the poem again. Invite the children to raise their hands each time they hear a word that begins with the same sound as **kitten**.

▶ Pronounce groups of words, two of which begin with the same sound. Ask the children to tell you which word begins with a different sound. Use these word sets: **kitten, kite, bee; girl, kind, good; hat, king, kernel; kangaroo, kick, dog; hill, hand, kindergarten; kitchen, fast, food; goose, keep, give; jump, kennel, kiss.**

ASSESS AND PLAN   p. Z19

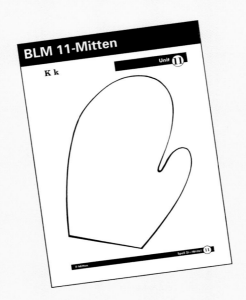

BLM 11-Mitten

K k

K k

Three Little Kittens

Three little kittens lost their mittens,
and they began to cry,
"Oh, mother dear, we sadly fear
Our mittens we have lost!"

"What! lost your mittens,
you naughty kittens!
Then you shall have no pie."
"Meow, meow, meow!"

The three little kittens found their mittens,
and they began to cry,
"Oh! mother dear, see here, see here,
Our mittens we have found."

"What! found your mittens,
you good little kittens,
Then you shall have some pie."
"Purr, purr, purr."

Three Little Kittens

Three little kittens lost their mittens,
and they began to cry,
"Oh, mother dear, we sadly fear
Our mittens we have lost!"

"What! lost your mittens,
you naughty kittens!
Then you shall have no pie."
"Meow, meow, meow!"

The three little kittens found their mittens,
and they began to cry,
"Oh! mother dear, see here, see here,
Our mittens we have found."

"What! found your mittens,
you good little kittens,
Then you shall have some pie."
"Purr, purr, purr."

Getting Ready to Teach

▶ Cut 10 to 12 mittens from construction paper or wallpaper samples using the pattern on BLM 11-Mitten.

ABC)) SOUND-SYMBOL AWARENESS

(pp. 66–67)

▶ Reread "Three Little Kittens" to the class.

▶ Write capital **K** and lowercase **k** on a wall chart. Identify the letter and tell the children it stands for the sound they hear at the beginning of **kitten**.

▶ Ask the children to repeat after you first the sound and then the letter several times: \k\, **k**.

▶ Help the children find pages 66 and 67. Ask them if they can find a kitten in the picture. Write **kitten** under **Kk** on the chart. Ask them what letter begins the word **kitten**. (Response: **k**)

▶ Ask the children to find other things in the picture whose names start with the same sound as **kitten**.

FYI Pictured words are listed at the bottom of the reduced student page.

▶ Prompt the children as needed. At first, you may wish to control the naming of the pictured words. For example, you may ask, *"Do you see a kite?"* and continue in this manner for each pictured word. (Later, the children will become more aggressive in finding picture names independently.)

▶ Write each word on the chart; say the word, emphasizing the beginning sound; and ask the children to repeat it. Ask what letter begins the word.

▶ Place the paper mittens around the classroom. Tell the children they can help the kittens find their mittens by saying words that begin with the same sound as **kitten**. Provide prompts and wait time as needed. As the children suggest appropriate words, allow them to claim a mitten. Add the children's responses to the wall chart. Continue the activity until all the mittens have been claimed.

FYI If children name words that begin with **c**, write these words on the wall chart in a separate column and explain that sometimes \k\ is spelled **c**.

◥ **ASSESS** AND **PLAN**   p. Z19

Kk

66   Unit II

Pictured Words
kittens, kick, kitchen, kite, king, key, koala, kangaroo, kettle

USING THE PICTURE-SORT CARDS

After the illustrations on pages 66 and 67 have been identified and discussed, consider using the *Picture-Sort Cards* for this unit. Possible activities include the following:

▶ Duplicate the *Picture-Sort Cards* for this unit and separate them. Distribute one set of cards to individuals or small groups. Say each pictured word aloud. Ask each student to place the pointer finger of his/her right hand on a *Picture-Sort Card* and then to place the pointer finger of his/her left hand on the matching picture in the illustration in their book. (Students working in groups can take turns.) Walk around to provide assistance and praise their efforts. Encourage children to talk about the pictures.

▶ Separate the *Picture-Sort Cards* and place them in an envelope in an activity center. Label the envelope with the targeted letter, e.g., **K**. Work with individuals or small groups to match each *Picture-Sort Card* with its corresponding picture in the illustration.

For more information on using *Picture-Sort Cards,* see the *Picture-Sort Card Book*.

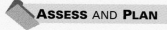

SPELLING PLUS

▶ Help the children find page 163.

▶ Ask them to find the letters **Kk**. Encourage them to draw a picture of something whose name begins with **k**, or provide old magazines from which they can cut appropriate pictures to glue beside the letters.

▶ You may wish to review words on the wall chart and suggest the children choose one of these to illustrate.

YOUR CHOICE:

SPELLING PLUS

▶ Cut ten pairs of mittens using the pattern on BLM 11-Mitten. On each left mitten, write a numeral from 1 to 10. On each right mitten, draw an appropriate number of dots or other simple figures, such as stars, hearts, flowers, fish, balls, diamonds, triangles, circles, and squares.

▶ Place the mittens in random order on the chalk tray. Challenge the children to match the mittens.

Diversity in Language and Culture

The letter **k** is a predictable letter in English. It stands for only one sound, although it is usually silent when it precedes **n**.

In English, \k\ is sometimes spelled **k** and sometimes **c** (as in **cat**).

The \k\ sound is represented by the letter **q** in words beginning with **qu**.

The \k\ sound belongs to the class of consonants known as stops because air is completely stopped as pressure builds in the mouth, and then the pressure is released suddenly, producing a sound. While \b\ and \p\ are stopped at the lips and \d\ and \t\ are stopped at the teeth, \k\ is stopped further back. The back of the tongue rises and blocks the air at the soft palate, or velum, of the roof of the mouth; \k\ is a velar stop. Its closest related sound is \g\, which is like \k\ except that the vocal cords are vibrating while the air is being released to produce \g\, while \k\ is voiceless.

One difference between \k\ in English and its counterpart in Spanish, French, and many other languages is that the English \k\ is accompanied by a puff of air (or aspiration) at the beginning of words. Sometimes nonnative English speakers pronounce \k\ without aspiration. Such a pronunciation sounds a bit like \g\ to a native English speaker.

HELPING STUDENTS ACQUIRING ENGLISH

Students benefit from the use of as many sensory experiences (hear, touch, feel, smell, taste) as possible. Bring into class some of the objects shown in the illustration on pages 66 and 67. (A kite, a key, and a stuffed kitten may be especially accessible. A ball will help illustrate **kick**.) Place them on a table and allow students to pick them up and say their names. Use gestures to illustrate some action words and say short sentences such as, *"I kick the ball." "I kiss the kitten." "I fly the kite."* Allow the students to illustrate the sentences with gestures.

TEMPORARY SPELLING

(p. 68)

▶ Direct the children's attention to the letter forms at the top of the page.

▶ Demonstrate the formation of capital **K** and lowercase **k**.

▶ Encourage the children to use this page in one of the following ways:

- to practice writing the letter forms;
- to draw one or more pictures of things whose names begin with the same sound as **kitten** and to label each picture;
- to write words that begin with **k**.

▶ Circulate to observe the children's efforts. Ask them to tell you about their drawing and writing.

▶ Accept temporary spellings.

YOUR CHOICE:

 SPELLING PLUS

| ▶ Invite the children to practice forming **K** and **k** using kernels of corn. Demonstrate the activity.

ASSESS AND **PLAN** p. Z19

 Letters and Words

K k

PERIOD 4

 INTERACTIVE WRITING

▶ Reread "Three Little Kittens" aloud.

▶ Ask the children to tell you something that happened in the poem. Write their responses in sentence form on strips of chart paper or tagboard.

▶ As you write, you may wish to invite the children to tell you the initial letter for words that begin with previously introduced sound-letter relationships (**a** through **k**). (Use your judgment to decide whether this activity is developmentally appropriate for your class at this time.)

▶ Read the sentence strips aloud and ask the children to tell you what happened first, second, third, and so on. Rearrange the sentences in order.

▶ Ask the children to find the letter **k** in the sentences.

YOUR CHOICE:

PERSONAL WRITING

▶ Ask the children how the kittens may have felt at different points in the poem. (Possible responses: sad, sorry, afraid, happy, relieved) Discuss other feelings.

▶ Invite the children to draw a face that shows a feeling.

▶ Encourage them to label their drawings or write about what might cause the feeling.

▶ Encourage temporary spellings.

▶ Allow time for sharing.

ASSESS AND **PLAN** p. Z19

My Writing

Emergent Spelling Notes

Like many children, Leslie experiences five stages of spelling development. Here is a sample of her spelling at the transitional stage.

Leslie's Writing

WONES A PON a time we BOTE a LITTEL kitten. You NO how THAY are WHIN THERE little—THERE RASCULES! This one LUVES to CLLIME trees and SRCACH PEPPEL. HE is a MENE RASCULE.

▶ Help the children find page 69.

▶ Choose one of the *Personal Writing Activities* (A–D) listed at the bottom of this page or offer the children a choice.

▶ Accept scribblings, random letters, and invented spellings.

▶ Allow time for the children to share their pictures and writing.

ASSESS AND **PLAN** p. Z19

Unit II (69)

PERSONAL WRITING ACTIVITIES

Activity A

▶ Encourage the children to write about what they like best about kindergarten and to illustrate their writing.

Activity B

▶ Discuss keys and their uses with the children. Ask them to name different kinds of keys. (Possible responses: house keys, car keys, piano keys, computer keys)

▶ Invite them to draw a picture of one or more keys and to label them or write something about them.

Activity C

▶ Invite the children to draw a picture of a kite and to write a story or poem about it.

Activity D

▶ Write *Be Kind to Kittens* on the chalkboard and tell the children to copy this title on page 69.

▶ Invite them to draw a picture of a kitten and the things they would need to take care of it.

▶ Encourage them to write a name for the kitten and to label the other things in their drawing.

ADDITIONAL LITERATURE

Fox, Mem. *Koala Lou*. Harcourt Brace Jovanovich, 1988.

Kanao, Keiko. *Kitten up a Tree*. Alfred A. Knopf/Borzoi Books, 1987.

McMillan, Bruce. *Kitten Can...A Concept Book*. Lothrop, 1984.

Polushkin, Maria. *Kitten in Trouble*. Bradbury Press, 1988.

GOALS

The children will

▶ develop phonemic awareness.

▶ identify words with the \l\ sound.

▶ associate \l\ with the letter l.

▶ engage in interactive writing.

▶ engage in personal writing.

▶ use invented spellings.

MATERIALS

Program materials you will need: student edition pages 70–75, *Assess and Plan File*

Optional materials: old magazines, scissors, glue, lace ribbon

PERIOD 1

Getting Ready to Teach

▶ Copy the poem from page T71 on chart paper.

Sharing the Poem (pp. 70–71)

▶ Help the children find pages 70 and 71.

▶ Read the poem to the class, pointing to the words as you read.

▶ Solicit personal responses to the poem. Use these responses and the illustration to guide a brief discussion of the poem.

))))))))))) PHONEMIC AWARENESS

▶ Ask the children to say the word **lamb** with you. Ask them what sound they hear at the beginning of **lamb**. (Response: \l\) Ask if anyone has a name that begins with this sound. (Possible responses: Luke, Laura, Larry, Linda)

▶ Read the poem again. Invite the children to raise their hands each time they hear a word that begins with the same sound as **lamb**.

▶ Encourage the children to look around the classroom for items whose names begin like **lamb**. (Possible responses: lights, letters, legs, lips)

▶ Tell the children they can make new words by adding \l\ to the beginning of words you say. Demonstrate by saying "**am, lamb**" and asking the children to repeat the words. Use these words: **ace** (**lace**), **aid** (**laid**), **and** (**land**), **ate** (**late**), **aw** (**law**), **earn** (**learn**), **east** (**least**), **edge** (**ledge**), **end** (**lend**), **it** (**lit**).

YOUR CHOICE:

 **SPELLING PLUS**

▶ Invite the children to bring a favorite stuffed animal or toy to show the class and talk about.

◢ **ASSESS** AND **PLAN**   p. Z19

Mary Had
a Little Lamb

Mary had a little lamb,
    Its fleece was white as snow;
And everywhere that Mary went
    The lamb was sure to go.

He followed her to school one day,
    Which was against the rule;
It made the children laugh and play
    To see a lamb at school.

SOUND-SYMBOL AWARENESS

(pp. 72–73)

▶ Reread "Mary Had a Little Lamb" to the class.

▶ Write capital **L** and lowercase **l** on a wall chart. Identify the letter and tell the children it stands for the sound they hear at the beginning of **lamb**.

▶ Ask the children to repeat after you first the sound and then the letter several times: \l\, l.

▶ Help the children find pages 72 and 73. Ask them if they can find a lamb in the picture. Write **lamb** under **Ll** on the chart. Ask them what letter begins the word **lamb**. (Response: **l**)

▶ Ask the children to find other things in the picture whose names start with the same sound as **lamb**.

FYI Pictured words are listed at the bottom of the reduced student page.

▶ Prompt the children as needed. At first, you may wish to control the naming of the pictured words. For example, you may ask, *"Do you see a ladder?"* and continue in this manner for each pictured word. (Later, the children will become more aggressive in finding picture names independently.)

▶ Write each word on the chart; say the word, emphasizing the beginning sound; and ask the children to repeat it. Ask what letter begins the word.

▶ Ask the children to generate other words that begin with the same sound as **lamb**. Provide prompts and wait time as needed. Add the children's responses to the wall chart.

72 Unit 12

Pictured Words
lamb, leash, lettuce, lightning, lemon, ladder, leaves, lion, lizard, lock, letter

 **ASSESS** AND **PLAN** p. Z19

USING THE PICTURE-SORT CARDS

After the illustrations on pages 72 and 73 have been identified and discussed, consider using the *Picture-Sort Cards* for this unit. Possible activities include the following:

▶ Duplicate the *Picture-Sort Cards* for this unit and separate them. Distribute one set of cards to individuals or small groups. Say each pictured word aloud. Ask each student to place the pointer finger of his/her right hand on a *Picture-Sort Card* and then to place the pointer finger of his/her left hand on the matching picture in the illustration in their book. (Students working in groups can take turns.) Walk around to provide assistance and praise their efforts. Encourage children to talk about the pictures.

▶ Separate the *Picture-Sort Cards* and place them in an envelope in an activity center. Label the envelope with the targeted letter, e.g., **L**. Work with individuals or small groups to match each *Picture-Sort Card* with its corresponding picture in the illustration.

For more information on using *Picture-Sort Cards,* see the *Picture-Sort Card Book.*

Unit 12 73

YOUR CHOICE:

SPELLING PLUS

▶ Help the children find page 164.

▶ Ask them to find the letters **Ll**. Encourage them to draw a picture of something whose name begins with **l**, or provide old magazines from which they can cut appropriate pictures to glue beside the letters.

▶ You may wish to review words on the wall chart and suggest the children choose one of these to illustrate.

Diversity in Language and Culture

The \l\ sound is spelled **l** and **ll**. This sound is a bit complicated to make, and children often have trouble with \l\ and \r\, which are somewhat related.

Some languages, including Japanese, don't have separate \l\ and \r\ sounds, and Japanese learners of English often confuse the two English sounds, both in listening and in speaking.

On the other hand, many languages do have the \l\ sound, and it is usually similar to the English sound. The biggest difference is usually how far toward the upper front teeth the tongue is placed.

The \l\ sound is often called a "liquid" consonant because of how it sounds rather than how it is made. Liquids are produced with very little friction and are much like vowel sounds.

You can hold \l\ just as you can hold a vowel sound. The \l\ sound is a lateral, or side, liquid because the tongue blocks the center of the mouth and the air passes over the sides of the tongue. To feel this, pronounce \l\; then, without moving your tongue, inhale and notice where the air rushes in.

Children who have trouble pronouncing \l\ will often substitute \w\ when first learning the liquid \l\.

HELPING STUDENTS ACQUIRING ENGLISH

Hands-on, visual activities help imprint letters and words in memory. Continually emphasize activities that require students to draw, cut out pictures, and engage in labeling. For example, the *Your Choice: Spelling Plus* activity on this page of the teacher edition is a good choice.

Validate students' primary language(s) by encouraging them to create another picture with an object that begins with the \l\ sound in their primary language(s). Have them label the picture with the letter **l**. From the words pictured on pages 72 and 73 of the student text, Spanish-speaking students might choose **limón** (**lemon**) or **león** (**lion**).

 **TEMPORARY SPELLING**

(p. 74)

▶ Direct the children's attention to the letter forms at the top of the page.

▶ Demonstrate the formation of capital **L** and lowercase **l**.

▶ Encourage the children to use this page in one of the following ways:

- to practice writing the letter forms;

- to draw one or more pictures of things whose names begin with the same sound as **lamb** and to label each picture;

- to write words that begin with **l**.

▶ Circulate to observe the children's efforts. Ask them to tell you about their drawing and writing.

▶ Accept temporary spellings.

YOUR CHOICE:

 SPELLING PLUS

▶ Invite the children to practice forming **L** and **l** using scraps of lace ribbon. Demonstrate the activity.

ASSESS AND **PLAN**　　　p. Z19

Letters and Words

L l

PERIOD 4

INTERACTIVE WRITING

▶ Reread "Mary Had a Little Lamb" aloud.

▶ Invite the children to tell you something they learned about the lamb. Write their responses in sentence form on chart paper.

▶ As you write, you may wish to invite the children to tell you the initial letter for words that begin with previously introduced sound-letter relationships (**a** through **l**). (Use your judgment to decide whether this activity is developmentally appropriate for your class at this time.)

YOUR CHOICE:

PERSONAL WRITING

▶ Invite the children to write a story about a pet that did something unusual. You may wish to suggest the children work on their stories with a partner. Invite them to illustrate their stories.

▶ Encourage temporary spellings.

▶ Allow time for sharing.

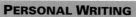 **ASSESS** AND **PLAN**　　　p. Z19

My Writing

Emergent Spelling Notes

Like many children, Leslie experiences five stages of spelling development. Here is a sample of her spelling at the conventional stage.

Leslie's Spelling

When I went to the zoo, I saw lions. They were sleeping. There were two of them. They were big and HARY.

PERSONAL WRITING   p. 75

▶ Help the children find page 75.

▶ Choose one of the *Personal Writing Activities* (A–D) listed at the bottom of this page or offer the children a choice.

▶ Accept scribblings, random letters, and invented spellings.

▶ Allow time for the children to share their pictures and writing.

ASSESS AND PLAN   p. Z19

PERSONAL WRITING ACTIVITIES

Activity A

▶ Write *Lunch List* on the chalkboard. Read the title and ask the children to copy it at the top of page 75.

▶ Ask them to write a list of their favorite things to eat for lunch.

▶ Encourage them to illustrate their lists.

Activity B

▶ Write *My Library* on the chalkboard. Read the title and ask the children to copy it at the top of page 75.

▶ Ask them to write a list of their favorite stories or picture books and to draw a picture illustrating one of them.

Activity C

▶ Write *Lulu's Laundry* on the chalkboard. Read the title and ask the children to write it at the top of page 75. Define **laundry**.

▶ Invite the children to draw the front of a laundromat around the title and to write an advertisement for the business.

Activity D

▶ Write **luggage** on the chalkboard. Read the word and define it.

▶ Invite the children to draw a picture of a piece of luggage and to make a list of the things they would put into it for a trip they would like to take.

▶ Encourage them to write a sentence about where they would go on their trip.

ADDITIONAL LITERATURE

Hoban, Tana. *Look! Look! Look!* Greenwillow Books, 1988.

Kraus, Robert. *Leo the Late Bloomer*. Harper & Row, 1987.

Krensky, Stephen. *Lionel at Large*. Dial Books for Young Readers, 1986.

G O A L S

The children will

▶ develop phonemic awareness.

▶ identify words with the \m\ sound.

▶ associate \m\ with the letter **m**.

▶ engage in interactive writing.

▶ engage in personal writing.

▶ use invented spellings.

M A T E R I A L S

Program materials you will need: student edition pages 76–81, *Assess and Plan File*, BLM 13-Miss Muffet

Other materials you will need: scissors

Optional materials: old magazines, glue, a box of uncooked macaroni noodles, musical selections on audiocassette, audiocassette player

P E R I O D   1

Getting Ready to Teach

▶ Copy the poem from page T77 on chart paper.

Sharing the Poem (pp. 76–77)

▶ Help the children find pages 76 and 77.

▶ Read the poem to the class, pointing to the words as you read.

▶ You may wish to tell the children that curds and whey is a food something like cottage cheese.

▶ Solicit personal responses to the poem. Use these responses and the illustration to guide a brief discussion of the poem.

▶ Group the children in pairs. Assign one child in each pair to be Miss Muffet and the other to be the spider. Explain and demonstrate the following movements to go with the lines of the poem:

• Lines 1–3: Miss Muffet pretends to eat the curds and whey.

• Lines 4–5: The spider wiggles its fingers toward Miss Muffet.

• Line 6: Miss Muffet gets up and runs away.

▶ Invite the children to recite the poem with you and use these actions to dramatize it.

PHONEMIC AWARENESS

▶ Ask the children to say the word **miss** with you. Ask them what sound they hear at the beginning of **miss**. (Response: \m\) Ask if anyone has a name that begins with this sound. (Possible responses: Midori, Maria, Manuel, Michael)

▶ Read the poem again. Invite the children to raise their hands each time they hear a word that begins with the same sound as **miss**.

▶ Encourage the children to look around the classroom for objects whose names begin like **miss**. (Possible responses: magazines, magnets, map, marbles, mats, metal, mouths)

▶ Distribute BLM 13-Miss Muffet. Ask the children to cut out the figures of Miss Muffet and the spider.

▶ Say **miss**. Ask these questions:

• Do you hear \m\? (Response: yes)

• Do you hear \m\ at the beginning or the end of **miss**? (Response: at the beginning)

▶ Ask the children to hold up Miss Muffet to show that \m\ is at the beginning of **miss**.

▶ Say **hum**. Ask these questions:

• Do you hear \m\? (Response: yes)

• Do you hear \m\ at the beginning or the end of **hum**? (Response: at the end)

▶ Ask the children to hold up the spider to show that \m\ is at the end of **hum**.

▶ If the children have trouble hearing \m\ at the end of **hum**, pronounce several more words ending with \m\. Draw out the final \m\ sound as you say the following words and ask the children to listen for \m\ at the end of each word: **lamb, ham, him, Tom, thumb**.

▶ Pronounce words that begin or end with \m\. Ask the children to hold up Miss Muffet if they hear \m\ at the beginning of the word and to hold up the spider if they hear \m\ at the end of the word. Use these words: **man, Sam, mad, came, make, name, time, mine, mud, come, mom**. (For **mom**, the children should hold up both Miss Muffet and the spider.)

ASSESS AND **PLAN**   p. Z19

BLM 13-Miss Muffet

Miss Muffet

Little Miss Muffet
Sat on a tuffet,
Eating of curds and whey;
There came a big spider,
And sat down beside her,
And frightened Miss Muffet away.

SOUND-SYMBOL AWARENESS
(pp. 78–79)

▶ Reread "Miss Muffet" to the class.

▶ Write capital **M** and lowercase **m** on a wall chart. Identify the letter and tell the children it stands for the sound they hear at the beginning of **miss**.

▶ Ask the children to repeat after you first the sound and then the letter several times: \m\, **m**.

▶ Help the children find pages 78 and 79. Ask them if they can find a monkey in the picture. Write **monkey** under **Mm** on the chart. Ask them what letter begins the word **monkey**. (Response: **m**)

▶ Ask the children to find other things in the picture whose names start with the same sound as **monkey**.

FYI Pictured words are listed at the bottom of the reduced student page.

▶ If you wish to control the naming of the pictured words, ask, *"Do you see a mop?"* and continue in this manner for each pictured word. If you want the children to initiate the naming of the pictures, provide prompts only as necessary.

▶ Write each word on the chart; say the word, emphasizing the beginning sound; and ask the children to repeat it. Ask what letter begins the word.

▶ Ask the children to generate other words that begin with the same sound as **monkey**. Provide prompts and wait time as needed. Add the children's responses to the wall chart.

◢ **ASSESS** AND **PLAN**　　　p. Z19

Mm

Pictured Words
monkey, moon, mountain, muffin, mailbox, mop, mouse, milk, motorcycle, mirror, magazines, marbles

USING THE PICTURE-SORT CARDS

After the illustrations on pages 78 and 79 have been identified and discussed, consider using the *Picture-Sort Cards* for this unit. Possible activities include the following:

▶ Duplicate the *Picture-Sort Cards* for this unit and separate them. Distribute one set of cards to individuals or small groups. Say each pictured word aloud. Ask each student to place the pointer finger of his/her right hand on a *Picture-Sort Card* and then to place the pointer finger of his/her left hand on the matching picture in the illustration in their book. (Students working in groups can take turns.) Walk around to provide assistance and praise their efforts. Encourage children to talk about the pictures.

▶ Separate the *Picture-Sort Cards* and place them in an envelope in an activity center. Label the envelope with the targeted letter, e.g., **M**. Work with individuals or small groups to match each *Picture-Sort Card* with its corresponding picture in the illustration.

For more information on using *Picture-Sort Cards,* see the *Picture-Sort Card Book.*

YOUR CHOICE:

 SPELLING PLUS

▶ Help the children find page 164.

▶ Ask them to find the letters **Mm.** Encourage them to draw a picture of something whose name begins with **m,** or provide old magazines from which they can cut appropriate pictures to glue beside the letters.

▶ You may wish to review words on the wall chart and suggest the children choose one of these to illustrate.

Diversity in Language and Culture

The \m\ sound is one children like to make and to play with. It is one of the most widespread sounds in languages around the world. Even languages with few distinct sounds have \m\. (The Hawaiian language has only thirteen sounds, but one of them is \m\.)

The \m\ sound is called a bilabial nasal stop, which means the lips are closed and air enters the nose while the vocal cords vibrate.

Related to \m\ are \p\ and \b\, the two oral bilabial stops, in which air is kept from entering the nose, and the nasal sound \n\, which is like \m\

except that \n\ blocks the air at the teeth rather than at the lips.

The letter **m** represents only the \m\ sound. The \m\ sound can be spelled **m, mm, lm (calm), mb (lamb),** and occasionally **mn (autumn).**

The old nursery rhyme "Miss Muffet" may be unfamiliar to some children in your class. When you discuss curds and whey, you might also talk about traditional foods of different cultures. Yogurt dishes, for example, are popular in some parts of the world, and there are many different kinds of cheeses around the world.

HELPING STUDENTS ACQUIRING ENGLISH

Several of the **m** words pictured on pages 78 and 79 name objects that also begin with **m** in Spanish, such as **mono (monkey), montaña (mountain), motocicleta (motorcycle).** Spanish-speaking students may also identify the table (**mesa**) as an **m** word. Ask students to identify other objects that also begin with the **m** sound in their primary language(s).

TEMPORARY SPELLING

(p. 80)

▶ Direct the children's attention to the letter forms at the top of the page.

▶ Demonstrate the formation of capital **M** and lowercase **m**.

▶ Encourage the children to use this page in one of the following ways:

- to practice writing the letter forms;

- to draw one or more pictures of things whose names begin with the same sound as **monkey** and to label each picture;

- to write words that begin with **m**.

▶ Circulate to observe the children's efforts. Ask them to tell you about their drawing and writing.

▶ Accept temporary spellings.

YOUR CHOICE:

SPELLING PLUS

▶ Invite the children to practice forming **M** and **m** using macaroni. Demonstrate the activity.

ASSESS AND **PLAN** p. Z19

Letters and Words

Mm

PERIOD 4

INTERACTIVE WRITING

▶ Reread "Miss Muffet" aloud.

▶ Ask the children to think of reasons Miss Muffet might have been frightened by the spider.

▶ Write their responses on chart paper in sentence form. As you write, you may wish to invite the children to tell you the initial letter for words that begin with previously introduced sound-letter relationships (**a** through **m**). (Use your judgment to decide whether this activity is developmentally appropriate for your class at this time.)

YOUR CHOICE:

PERSONAL WRITING

▶ Ask the children to think of another animal or thing that might frighten a person and to draw a picture of the frightening object.

▶ Invite them to label their drawings or write something about them.

▶ Encourage temporary spellings.

▶ Allow time for sharing.

ASSESS AND **PLAN** p. Z19

My Writing

Emergent Spelling Notes

Dan's grocery list reads "milk, bran flakes, dough-nuts." Note that at this early stage, Dan did not know that letters represent sounds. He did not yet understand the alphabetic principle.

EOOS
FISOS
MSOOE

PERSONAL WRITING   p. 81

- Help the children find page 81.
- Choose one of the *Personal Writing Activities* (A–D) listed at the bottom of this page or offer the children a choice.
- Accept scribblings, random letters, and invented spellings.
- Allow time for the children to share their pictures and writing.

ASSESS AND **PLAN**   p. Z19

PERSONAL WRITING ACTIVITIES

Activity A

- Play musical selections and ask the children to think about how the music makes them feel.
- Encourage them to illustrate the music and write how it makes them feel.

Activity B

- Write *At the Market* on the chalkboard. Read the title and ask the children to copy it at the top of page 81.
- Encourage the children to draw pictures of things that can be found in a market and to label their pictures or write something about going to the market.

- You may wish to provide a list of market items whose names begin with **m**: milk, meat, melons, marshmallows, macaroni, mixes.

Activity C

- Invite the children to draw a street map. Suggest they label the streets on their map with names that begin with **m**.

Activity D

- Invite the children to draw a monster and give it a name that starts with **m**.
- Encourage them to write what their monster likes to eat or what it likes to do for fun.

ADDITIONAL LITERATURE

Cole, Joanna. *The Missing Tooth*. Random House, 1988.

Gibbons, Gail. *The Milk Makers*. Macmillan, 1985.

McKissack, Patricia. *Monkey-Monkey's Trick: Based on an African Folk Tale*. Random House, 1988.

Polushkin, Maria. *Who Said Meow?* Bradbury Press, 1988.

Wiseman, Bernard. *Morris the Moose*. Harper & Row, 1989.

G O A L S

The children will

▶ develop phonemic awareness.

▶ identify words with the \n\ sound.

▶ associate \n\ with the letter **n**.

▶ engage in interactive writing.

▶ engage in personal writing.

▶ use invented spellings.

M A T E R I A L S

Program materials you will need: student edition pages 82–87, *Assess and Plan File,* BLM 14-Net and Ten

Other materials you will need: scissors

Optional materials: old magazines, glue, uncooked noodles

P E R I O D 1

Getting Ready to Teach

▶ Copy the poem from page T83 on chart paper.

Sharing the Poem (pp. 82–83)

▶ Help the children find pages 82 and 83.

▶ Read the poem to the class, pointing to the words as you read.

▶ Solicit personal responses to the poem. Use these responses and the illustration to guide a brief discussion of the poem.

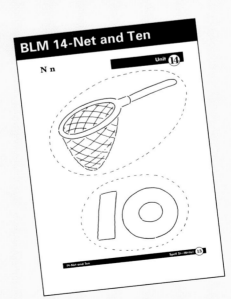

**PHONEMIC AWARENESS**

▶ Ask the children to say the word **nine** with you. Ask them what sound they hear at the beginning of **nine.** (Response: \n\) Ask them what sound they hear at the end of **nine.** (Response: \n\) Ask if anyone has a name that begins with this sound. (Possible responses: Nancy, Natalie, Nathan, Nicholas)

▶ Read the poem again. Invite the children to raise their hands each time they hear a word that begins with the same sound as **nine.**

▶ Encourage the children to look around the classroom for objects whose names begin like **nine.** (Possible responses: nails, necklace, necks, noses, numbers)

▶ Distribute BLM 14-Net and Ten and ask the children to cut out the net and the numeral 10.

▶ Say **net.** Ask these questions:

• Do you hear \n\? (Response: yes)

• Do you hear \n\ at the beginning or the end of **net**? (Response: at the beginning)

▶ Ask the children to hold up the picture of the net to show that \n\ is at the beginning of **net.**

▶ Say **ten.** Ask these questions:

• Do you hear \n\? (Response: yes)

• Do you hear \n\ at the beginning or the end of **ten**? (Response: at the end)

▶ Ask the children to hold up the numeral 10 to show that \n\ is at the end of **ten.**

▶ If the children have trouble hearing \n\ at the end of **ten,** pronounce several more words ending with \n\. Draw out the final \n\ sound as you say the following words and ask the children to listen for \n\ at the end of each word: **man, fun, rain, June, then.**

▶ Pronounce words that begin or end with \n\. Ask the children to hold up the picture of the net if they hear \n\ at the beginning of the word and to hold up the numeral 10 if they hear \n\ at the end of the word. Use these words: **nap, ran, nose, soon, name, never, win, mine, nice, bone, need.**

◥ **ASSESS** AND **PLAN**　　p. Z19

Big N, Little n

BIG N

little n

What begins with those?

Nine new neckties
and a nightshirt
and a nose.

—Dr. Seuss

SOUND-SYMBOL AWARENESS
(pp. 84–85)

▶ Reread "Big N, Little n" to the class.

▶ Write capital **N** and lowercase **n** on a wall chart. Identify the letter and tell the children it stands for the sound they hear at the beginning and end of **nine**.

▶ Ask the children to repeat after you first the sound and then the letter several times: \n\, **n**.

▶ Help the children find pages 84 and 85. Ask them if they can find the number 9 in the picture. Write **nine** under **Nn** on the chart. Ask them what letter begins the word **nine**. (Response: **n**)

▶ Ask the children to find other things in the picture whose names start with the same sound as **nine**.

FYI Pictured words are listed at the bottom of the reduced student page.

▶ If you wish to control the naming of the pictured words, ask, *"Do you see a net?"* and continue in this manner for each pictured word. If you want the children to initiate the naming of the pictures, provide prompts only as necessary.

▶ Write each word on the chart; say the word, emphasizing the beginning sound; and ask the children to repeat it. Ask what letter begins the word.

▶ Ask the children to generate other words that begin with the same sound as **nine**. Provide prompts and wait time as needed. Add the children's responses to the wall chart.

ASSESS AND **PLAN**   p. Z19

USING THE PICTURE-SORT CARDS

After the illustrations on pages 84 and 85 have been identified and discussed, consider using the *Picture-Sort Cards* for this unit. Possible activities include the following:

▶ Duplicate the *Picture-Sort Cards* for this unit and separate them. Distribute one set of cards to individuals or small groups. Say each pictured word aloud. Ask each student to place the pointer finger of his/her right hand on a *Picture-Sort Card* and then to place the pointer finger of his/her left hand on the matching picture in the illustration in their book. (Students working in groups can take turns.) Walk around to provide assistance and praise their efforts. Encourage children to talk about the pictures.

▶ Separate the *Picture-Sort Cards* and place them in an envelope in an activity center. Label the envelope with the targeted letter, e.g., **N**. Work with individuals or small groups to match each *Picture-Sort Card* with its corresponding picture in the illustration.

For more information on using *Picture-Sort Cards,* see the *Picture-Sort Card Book.*

84   Unit 14

Pictured Words
notebook, nine, net, nail, nuts, newspaper, nest, napkin, necklace, nurse, nutcracker

Unit 14   **85**

YOUR CHOICE:

SPELLING PLUS

▶ Help the children find page 164.

▶ Ask them to find the letters **Nn**. Encourage them to draw a picture of something whose name begins with **n,** or provide old magazines from which they can cut appropriate pictures to glue beside the letters.

▶ You may wish to review words on the wall chart and suggest the children choose one of these to illustrate.

Diversity in Language and Culture

The **n**\ sound is easy for children to make, and they learn to make it at a young age. It is one of the most widespread sounds in languages around the world. Even languages with few distinct sounds have **n**\. (The Hawaiian language has only 13 sounds, but one of them is **n**\.)

The **n**\ sound is called a nasal dental stop because the tongue blocks the air from exiting the mouth behind the upper front teeth, and the air is let into the nose while the vocal cords vibrate. Related to **n**\ are **t**\ and **d**\, the two oral dental stops (in which air is kept from entering the nose), and the nasal sound **m**\, which is like **n**\ except **n**\ blocks the air at the teeth while **m**\ blocks the air at the lips.

HELPING STUDENTS ACQUIRING ENGLISH

After the class has practiced a choral reading of the poem "Big N, Little n" (page 82), ask the students to work with an English-speaking study buddy to practice reading the poem aloud together. First the English-speaking student will read a line, and the student who is acquiring English will repeat the line. Then each student will read alternate lines, switch, and read the opposite lines. Finally, each student will attempt to read the poem alone.

PERIOD 3

 TEMPORARY SPELLING

(p. 86)

▶ Direct the children's attention to the letter forms at the top of the page.

▶ Demonstrate the formation of capital **N** and lowercase **n**.

▶ Encourage the children to use this page in one of the following ways:

- to practice writing the letter forms;
- to draw one or more pictures of things whose names begin with the same sound as **nine** and to label each picture;
- to write words that begin with **n**.

▶ Circulate to observe the children's efforts. Ask them to tell you about their drawing and writing.

▶ Accept temporary spellings.

YOUR CHOICE:

 SPELLING PLUS

▶ Invite the children to practice forming **N** and **n** using uncooked noodles. Demonstrate the activity.

◣ **ASSESS** AND **PLAN**   **p. Z19**

Letters and Words

Nn

PERIOD 4

INTERACTIVE WRITING

▶ Reread "Big N, Little n" aloud.

▶ Write "I have a..." on chart paper. Ask the children to help you finish the sentence using a word that starts with **n**. (Possible responses: **name, nose, neck, napkin, newspaper, nickel, nickname**) Write their responses in sentence form.

YOUR CHOICE:

PERSONAL WRITING

▶ Invite the children to choose one of the sentences on the chart and to expand it by writing more details or by using it as the beginning of a story.

▶ Encourage them to use their imaginations and to illustrate their writing.

▶ Encourage temporary spellings.

▶ Allow time for sharing.

◣ **ASSESS** AND **PLAN**   **p. Z19**

My Writing

Emergent Spelling Notes

The drawings are titled "Ideas of Quilts." Semiphonetic spellers begin to conceptualize that letters represent the sounds in words.

IDSAVCWLS

PERSONAL WRITING   p. 87

▶ Help the children find page 87.

▶ Choose one of the *Personal Writing Activities* (A–D) listed at the bottom of this page or offer the children a choice.

▶ Accept scribblings, random letters, and invented spellings.

▶ Allow time for the children to share their pictures and writing.

ASSESS AND PLAN   p. Z19

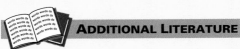

PERSONAL WRITING ACTIVITIES

Activity A

▶ Ask the children to write the numeral 9 at the top of page 87.

▶ Challenge them to draw nine pictures of things whose names begin with **n**. (They may draw nine of the same thing or nine different things.)

Activity B

▶ Share *Naughty Nancy Goes to School* with the children. (See *Additional Literature*.)

▶ Encourage the children to draw a picture about something in the story and to write something about the picture.

Activity C

▶ Discuss neighborhoods with the children. Invite them to draw a picture of the neighborhood they live in.

▶ Encourage them to write something about their neighborhood.

Activity D

▶ Write *Nice Noise* on the chalkboard. Read the title and ask the children to copy it at the top of page 87.

▶ Invite the children to write a description of their favorite kind of noise and to illustrate their writing.

ADDITIONAL LITERATURE

dePaola, Tomie. *Nana Upstairs and Nana Downstairs.* Putnam, 1987.

Goodall, John. *Naughty Nancy Goes to School.* McElderry/Macmillan, 1985.

Hayes, Sarah. *Nine Ducks Nine.* Lothrop, 1990.

Wells, Rosemary. *Noisy Nora.* Dial Books for Young Readers, 1973.

G O A L S

The children will

▶ develop phonemic awareness.

▶ identify words with the **short o** sound.

▶ associate the **short o** sound with the letter **o**.

▶ engage in interactive writing.

▶ engage in personal writing.

▶ use invented spellings.

M A T E R I A L S

Program materials you will need: student edition pages 88–93, *Assess and Plan File*, BLM 15-Octopus

Optional materials: old magazines, scissors, glue, dry oatmeal

P E R I O D 1

Getting Ready to Teach

▶ Copy the poem from page T89 on chart paper.

Sharing the Poem (pp. 88–89)

▶ Help the children find pages 88 and 89.

▶ Read the poem to the class, pointing to the words as you read.

▶ Solicit personal responses to the poem. Use these responses and the illustration to guide a brief discussion of the poem.

)))) PHONEMIC AWARENESS

▶ Ask the children to say the word **octopus** with you. Ask them what sound they hear at the beginning of **octopus**. (Response: \ah\) Ask if anyone has a name that begins with this sound. (Possible responses: Oscar, Otto, Olive, Octavia)

▶ Read the poem again. Invite the children to raise their hands each time they hear a word that begins with the same sound as **octopus**.

▶ Display the head of Ollie Octopus from BLM 15-Octopus. Tell the children you will say a word in slow motion and ask them to say it in a normal way. For example, if you say **got** as \g\-\ah\-\t\, the children should respond "got." Each time they say a word correctly, draw a tentacle on Ollie Octopus. Challenge the children to give Ollie more than eight tentacles.

▶ Use words that have a **short o** sound and only two or three phonemes, such as **odd, Oz, pop, hot, lock, not, hop, lot, top, rock, doll, mop, sock, pot, job**.

◤ **ASSESS** AND **PLAN**　　　p. **Z19**

Silly Ollie Octopus

Silly Ollie Octopus
Was putting on his sweater.
It's rather odd that he was cold,
Perhaps it was the weather.

"Come on, you silly octopus,
It's almost time to leave!"
But Ollie Octopus got left—
He couldn't find his sleeves!

—J. Richard Gentry

Silly Ollie Octopus

Silly Ollie Octopus
Was putting on his sweater.
It's rather odd that he was cold,
Perhaps it was the weather.

"Come on, you silly octopus,
It's almost time to leave!"
But Ollie Octopus got left—
He couldn't find his sleeves!

—J. Richard Gentry

 SOUND-SYMBOL AWARENESS

(pp. 90–91)

▶ Reread "Silly Ollie Octopus" to the class.

▶ Write capital **O** and lowercase **o** on a wall chart. Identify the letter and tell the children it stands for the sound they hear at the beginning of **octopus**.

▶ Ask the children to repeat after you first the sound and then the letter several times: \ah\, **o**.

▶ Help the children find pages 90 and 91. Ask them if they can find an octopus in the picture. Write **octopus** under **Oo** on the chart. Ask them what letter begins the word **octopus**. (Response: **o**)

▶ Ask the children to find other things in the picture whose names start with the same sound as **octopus**.

FYI Pictured words are listed at the bottom of the reduced student page.

▶ If you wish to control the naming of the pictured words, ask, *"Do you see an ox?"* and continue in this manner for each pictured word. If you want the children to initiate the naming of the pictures, provide prompts only as necessary.

▶ Write each word on the chart; say the word, emphasizing the beginning **short o** sound; and ask the children to repeat it. Ask what letter begins the word.

▶ Ask the children to generate other words that begin with the same sound as **octopus**. Provide prompts and wait time as needed. Add the children's responses to the wall chart.

90   Unit 15

Pictured Words

short o: octopus, ostrich, otter, ox, olives

long o: ocean, overalls, oatmeal

YOUR CHOICE:

 SPELLING PLUS

▶ If you wish to introduce **long o,** write **ocean** on a wall chart. Say the word and ask the children to repeat it. Ask them what sound they hear at the beginning of **ocean.** (Response: \oh\) Ask what letter begins the word **ocean.** (Response: **o**)

▶ Ask the children if they can find anything in the picture on pages 90 and 91 whose name begins with the same sound as **ocean.** Elicit responses as you did for words beginning with the **short o** sound.

▶ Write each word on the chart; say the word, emphasizing the **long o** sound; and ask the children to repeat it.

▶ Ask the children to generate other words that begin with the same sound as **ocean.** Provide prompts and wait time as needed. Add responses to the wall chart.

◢ **ASSESS** AND **PLAN**   **p. Z19**

USING THE PICTURE-SORT CARDS

After the illustrations on pages 90 and 91 have been identified and discussed, consider using the *Picture-Sort Cards* for this unit. For more information on using *Picture-Sort Cards*, see page T84 or the *Picture-Sort Card Book*.

YOUR CHOICE:

 **SPELLING PLUS**

▶ Help the children find page 165.

▶ Ask them to find the letters **Oo.** Encourage them to draw a picture of something whose name begins with **o,** or provide old magazines from which they can cut appropriate pictures to glue beside the letters.

▶ You may wish to review words on the wall chart and suggest the children choose one of these to illustrate.

Diversity in Language and Culture

The letter **o** stands for several different vowel sounds. This unit focuses primarily on the **short o** sound, as in **octopus,** and notes the **long o** sound, as in **ocean**.

The letter **o** always stands for a vowel sound. Vowel sounds are made by vibrating the vocal cords and changing the position of the tongue and the shape of the mouth to vary the sound. They are described in relation to how high or low the jaw is and how near the tongue is to the front or back of the mouth.

Both the **short o** and **long o** sounds are back vowels, meaning that the tongue is pushed back in the mouth. (Compare the back position of the tongue in **oh** with the position of the tongue in **eat,** which has a front vowel.) The jaw is open midway for **ocean** and drops more for **octopus,** which is a low vowel for most American English speakers.

Vowel sounds differ from region to region. The major variation in the **short o** sound has to do with how low the jaw drops, but this shouldn't cause any special problems in teaching words with the **short o** sound.

HELPING STUDENTS ACQUIRING ENGLISH

Ask students questions based on the poem "Silly Ollie Octopus" that simply require a "yes" or "no" answer. For example, you might ask:

• Was Ollie putting on his sweater? (Response: yes)

• Did Ollie get left because he couldn't find his olives? (no)

• Was Ollie left because he couldn't find his overalls? (no)

• Was Ollie left because he couldn't find his sleeves? (yes)

Next, change the questions so that they need only a one-word answer. For example:

• What was Ollie putting on? (sweater)

• What couldn't Ollie find? (sleeves)

TEMPORARY SPELLING

(p. 92)

▶ Direct the children's attention to the letter forms at the top of the page.

▶ Demonstrate the formation of capital **O** and lowercase **o**.

▶ Encourage the children to use this page in one of the following ways:

- to practice writing the letter forms;

- to draw one or more pictures of things whose names begin with the same sound as **octopus** and to label each picture;

- to write words that begin with **o**.

▶ Circulate to observe the children's efforts. Ask them to tell you about their drawing and writing.

▶ Accept temporary spellings.

YOUR CHOICE:

 SPELLING PLUS

▶ Invite the children to practice forming **O** and **o** using dry oatmeal and glue. Demonstrate the activity.

ASSESS AND PLAN　　　p. Z19

 **Letters and Words**

Oo

ASSESS AND PLAN　　　p. Z19

INTERACTIVE WRITING

▶ Reread "Silly Ollie Octopus" aloud.

▶ Ask the children to recall something about Ollie Octopus from the poem.

▶ Write their responses on chart paper in sentence form. As you write, you may wish to invite the children to tell you the initial letter for words that begin with previously introduced sound-letter relationships (**a** through **o**). (Use your judgment to decide whether this activity is developmentally appropriate for your class at this time.)

YOUR CHOICE:

PERSONAL WRITING

▶ Remind the children that Ollie Octopus had trouble putting on his sweater. Ask volunteers to tell about something they find difficult to do or something they once found difficult to do but can now do easily. Such activities might include tying shoelaces, riding a bicycle, blowing bubbles with bubble gum, fastening zippers.

▶ Invite the children to draw a picture of the activity and write something about it.

▶ Encourage temporary spellings.

▶ Allow time for sharing.

My Writing

Emergent Spelling Notes

Story writing with invented spelling helps set the foundations for later spelling competency. This story by Dan includes semiphonetic spelling.

If I had a magic pair of boots, I would make gold. (24 crts).

I would blo' up the shoole.

I would play football.

I would redd clifford books.

I would biy a camr.

Unit 15 **93**

 PERSONAL WRITING p. 93

▶ Help the children find page 93.

▶ Choose one of the *Personal Writing Activities* (A–D) listed at the bottom of this page or offer the children a choice.

▶ Accept scribblings, random letters, and invented spellings.

▶ Allow time for the children to share their pictures and writing.

ASSESS AND **PLAN** p. Z19

 PERSONAL WRITING ACTIVITIES

Activity A

▶ Invite the children to write a story about Ollie Octopus. You may wish to have them work in pairs or small groups. Encourage them to illustrate their stories.

Activity B

▶ Discuss October, its weather, and its special days with the children. Write *October* on the chalkboard and ask the children to copy the word at the top of page 93.

▶ Invite them to draw a picture of an October scene or special day.

▶ Encourage them to label the picture or write something about it.

Activity C

▶ Discuss opposites with the children. Write *Opposites* on the chalkboard and ask them to copy it at the top of page 93.

▶ Invite the children to draw pictures of opposites and to label their pictures or write something about them.

Activity D

▶ Invite the children to write a description of an object without actually naming it.

▶ Encourage them to read the description to a partner and ask the partner to guess what the object is.

ADDITIONAL LITERATURE

Brandenberg, Franz. *Otto Is Different.* Greenwillow Books, 1985.

Burton, Marilee Robin. *Oliver's Birthday.* Harper & Row, 1986.

Coats, Laura Jane. *The Oak Tree.* Macmillan, 1987.

Wadsworth, Olive A. *Over in the Meadow.* Scholastic Inc., 1988.

G O A L S

The children will

▶ develop phonemic awareness.

▶ identify words with the **p**\ sound.

▶ associate **p**\ with the letter **p**.

▶ engage in interactive writing.

▶ engage in personal writing.

▶ use invented spellings.

M A T E R I A L S

Program materials you will need: student edition pages 94–99, *Assess and Plan File,* BLM 16-Peter

Other materials you will need: scissors

Optional program materials: BLM 16-Picnic/Pocket

Other optional materials: green, red, yellow, and mild chili peppers, old magazines, glue, pipe cleaners or popped popcorn, crayons

PERIOD 1

Getting Ready to Teach

▶ Copy the poem from page T95 on chart paper.

Sharing the Poem (pp. 94–95)

▶ Help the children find pages 94 and 95.

▶ Read the poem to the class, pointing to the words as you read.

▶ Solicit personal responses to the poem. Use these responses and the illustration to guide a brief discussion of the poem.

▶ If possible, show samples of peppers to the class. Slice them and allow the children to taste them if they wish.

▶ Suggest to the children that they might recite the poem using the names of other vegetables and fruits whose names begin with **p**\. Ask the children for suggestions. (Possible responses: pineapples, pumpkins, potatoes, peaches, peas, pears, pickles)

▶ Conduct a choral reading of the poem, substituting the name of a fruit or vegetable of the children's choice for **peppers**.

)))) PHONEMIC AWARENESS

▶ Ask the children to say the word **pick** with you. Ask them what sound they hear at the beginning of **pick**. (Response: **p**\) Ask if anyone has a name that begins with this sound. (Possible responses: Patricia, Pamela, Pedro, Penny, Patrick, Paul)

▶ Read the poem again. Invite the children to raise their hands each time they hear a word that begins with the same sound as **pick**.

▶ Encourage the children to look around the classroom for objects whose names begin like **pick**. (Possible responses: pages, pail, paint, pants, paper, paste, pencils, people, piano, pictures, pockets, poster, pupils, puzzles, puppet)

▶ Distribute BLM 16-Peter. Ask the children to cut out the figures of Peter and the cap.

▶ Say **pick**. Ask these questions:
  • Do you hear **p**\? (Response: yes)
  • Do you hear **p**\ at the beginning or the end of **pick**? (Response: at the beginning)

▶ Ask the children to hold up Peter to show that **p**\ is at the beginning of **pick**.

▶ Say **cap**. Ask these questions:
  • Do you hear **p**\? (Response: yes)
  • Do you hear **p**\ at the beginning or the end of **cap**? (Response: at the end)

▶ Ask the children to hold up the cap to show that **p**\ is at the end of **cap**.

▶ If the children have trouble hearing **p**\ at the end of **cap**, pronounce several more words ending with **p**\. Emphasize the final **p**\ sound as you say the following words and ask the children to listen for **p**\ at the end of each word: **cup, hop, soap, clap, skip.**

▶ Pronounce words that begin or end with **p**\. Ask the children to hold up Peter if they hear **p**\ at the beginning and to hold up the cap if they hear **p**\ at the end. Use these words: **pat, tap, nip, pin, pet, step, pill, lip, top, pot, pop.** (For **pop,** the children should hold up both Peter and the cap.)

◣ ASSESS AND PLAN   p. Z19

BLM 16-Peter

BLM 16-Picnic/Pocket

Peter Piper

Peter Piper picked a peck of pickled peppers;
Did Peter Piper pick a peck of pickled peppers?
If Peter Piper picked a peck of pickled peppers,
Where's the peck of pickled peppers Peter Piper picked?

—Anonymous

94   Unit 16

Unit 16   95

Peter Piper

Peter Piper picked a peck of pickled peppers;
Did Peter Piper pick a peck of pickled peppers?
If Peter Piper picked a peck of pickled peppers,
Where's the peck of pickled peppers Peter Piper picked?

—Anonymous

SOUND-SYMBOL AWARENESS

(pp. 96–97)

▶ Reread "Peter Piper" to the class.

▶ Write capital **P** and lowercase **p** on a wall chart. Identify the letter and tell the children it stands for the sound they hear at the beginning of **Peter** and **pick**.

▶ Ask the children to repeat after you first the sound and then the letter several times: \p\, **p**.

▶ Help the children find pages 96 and 97. Ask them if they can find a pumpkin in the picture. Write **pumpkin** under **Pp** on the chart. Ask them what letter begins the word **pumpkin**. (Response: **p**)

▶ Ask the children to find other things in the picture whose names start with the same sound as **Peter, pick,** and **pumpkin**.

FYI Pictured words are listed at the bottom of the reduced student page.

▶ If you wish to control the naming of the pictured words, ask, *"Do you see a pony?"* and continue in this manner for each pictured word. If you want the children to initiate the naming of the pictures, provide prompts only as necessary.

▶ Write each word on the chart; say the word, emphasizing the beginning sound; and ask the children to repeat it. Ask what letter begins the word.

▶ Ask the children to generate other words that begin with the same sound as **Peter, pick,** and **pumpkin**. Provide prompts and wait time as needed. Add the children's responses to the wall chart.

96 Unit 16

Pictured Words

pumpkin, pencil, pig, pony, pepper, penny, peanut, paint, popcorn, puppet, puppy, picture

ASSESS AND PLAN   p. Z19

USING THE PICTURE-SORT CARDS

After the illustrations on pages 96 and 97 have been identified and discussed, consider using the *Picture-Sort Cards* for this unit. Possible activities include the following:

▶ Duplicate the *Picture-Sort Cards* for this unit and separate them. Distribute one set of cards to individuals or small groups. Say each pictured word aloud. Ask each student to place the pointer finger of his/her right hand on a *Picture-Sort Card* and then to place the pointer finger of his/her left hand on the matching picture in the illustration in their book. (Students working in

groups can take turns.) Walk around to provide assistance and praise their efforts. Encourage children to talk about the pictures.

▶ Separate the *Picture-Sort Cards* and place them in an envelope in an activity center. Label the envelope with the targeted letter, e.g., **P**. Work with individuals or small groups to match each *Picture-Sort Card* with its corresponding picture in the illustration.

For more information on using *Picture-Sort Cards,* see the *Picture-Sort Card Book.*

YOUR CHOICE:

   **SPELLING PLUS**

▶ Help the children find page 165.

▶ Ask them to find the letters **Pp**. Encourage them to draw a picture of something whose name begins with **p**, or provide old magazines from which they can cut appropriate pictures to glue beside the letters.

▶ You may wish to review words on the wall chart and suggest the children choose one of these to illustrate.

Diversity in Language and Culture

The \p\ sound is always spelled with **p**. The letter **p** represents a common sound in languages around the world. It is also one of the first sounds babies produce.

Technically, \p\ is a voiceless bilabial stop: the lips are closed, air pressure builds in the mouth, and then the lips are opened suddenly, releasing the air. Related sounds are \b\, a voiced bilabial, and \m\, a voiced nasal.

All these sounds are common, though some languages do not have all three. Arabic, for instance, has \b\, but \p\ as such really doesn't exist. (Arabic speakers are likely to pronounce **plastic** as \bi-las-tik\.) Korean \p\ is pronounced like \b\ between vowels,

but otherwise, there is no \b\ sound in Korean and a symbol to represent \b\ does not exist in the Korean writing system.

One difference between \p\ in English and in Spanish, French, and some other languages is that the English \p\ is pronounced with a puff of air (or aspiration), similar to \h\. Sometimes nonnative speakers of English pronounce English \p\ without the aspiration, and to native English speakers, this sounds a bit like \b\. If you hold a thin sheet of paper close to your lips and pronounce **pit** and then **bit,** you should see the paper flutter more with the aspirated \p\ of **pit** than with the unaspirated \b\ of **bit.**

**HELPING STUDENTS
ACQUIRING ENGLISH**

Plan a Family Day, inviting parents and other members of students' families to visit your classroom and to share information about their languages and their cultures. The plan might take the form of a luncheon in which family members bring dishes typical of their countries of origin.

Ask students if they know any tongue twisters in their primary language(s). Ask them to say the tongue twisters for the class. Ask parents visiting your class to translate the meanings of the tongue twisters.

TEMPORARY SPELLING

(p. 98)

▶ Direct the children's attention to the letter forms at the top of the page.

▶ Demonstrate the formation of capital **P** and lowercase **p**.

▶ Encourage the children to use this page in one of the following ways:

  • to practice writing the letter forms;

  • to draw one or more pictures of things whose names begin with the same sound as **Peter, pick,** and **pumpkin** and to label each picture;

  • to write words that begin with **p**.

▶ Circulate to observe the children's efforts. Ask them to tell you about their drawing and writing.

▶ Accept temporary spellings.

YOUR CHOICE:

SPELLING PLUS

▶ Invite the children to practice forming **P** and **p** using pipe cleaners or popped corn. Demonstrate the activity.

 ASSESS AND **PLAN**   **p. Z19**

Letters and Words

P p

PERIOD 4

INTERACTIVE WRITING

▶ Reread "Peter Piper" aloud.

▶ Invite the children to make up people's names in which both the first and last names begin with \p\. Write their responses on the chalkboard. Then ask them to think of something to say about each person using words that begin with \p\. You might wish to provide these examples to stimulate the children's thinking:

  • Paula Popper patted pigs.

  • Penny Poppins peddled pots and pans.

  • Pepe Peppel pitched perfectly.

YOUR CHOICE:

PERSONAL WRITING

▶ Suggest to the children that Peter Piper must like pickled peppers a great deal to have picked so many.

▶ Invite the children to draw a picture of their favorite food. Encourage them to label the picture or write something about it.

▶ Encourage temporary spellings.

▶ Allow time for sharing.

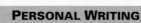 **ASSESS** AND **PLAN**   **p. Z19**

My Writing

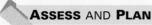

Emergent Spelling Notes

Story writing with invented spelling helps set the foundations for later spelling competency. This story by Dan includes semiphonetic spelling.

I would go to New york and see the Stabu of libtei

I would go out west.

I'd go to the grand canyn and biy a slatiti • (stalactite).

I would taked trip down the colordorrevre on a raft.

▶ Help the children find page 99.

▶ Choose one of the *Personal Writing Activities* (A–D) listed at the bottom of this page or offer the children a choice.

▶ Accept scribblings, random letters, and invented spellings.

▶ Allow time for the children to share their pictures and writing.

ASSESS AND **PLAN**   p. Z19

PERSONAL WRITING ACTIVITIES

Activity A

▶ Ask the children to draw a picture of something real or make-believe using only pink and purple crayons.

▶ Encourage them to label the picture or write something that tells what it is.

Activity B

▶ Distribute BLM 16-Picnic/Pocket and ask the children to color the picnic basket, cut it out, and glue it on page 99.

▶ Discuss supplies needed for a picnic. Ask the children to draw or cut from magazines pictures of things they would pack in the picnic basket.

▶ Encourage the children to write something about a picnic.

Activity C

▶ Distribute BLM 16-Picnic/Pocket and ask the children to color the pocket, cut it out, and glue it on page 99.

▶ Invite the children to draw pictures of things they put in their pockets.

▶ Encourage them to label their drawings or write something about them.

Activity D

▶ Write *The Perfect Pet* on the chalkboard. Read the title and ask the children to copy it at the top of page 99.

▶ Invite them to write a description of the perfect pet. Encourage them to illustrate their writing.

ADDITIONAL LITERATURE

Ahlberg, Janet and Allan. *Each Peach Pear Plum*. Viking, 1979.

Brown, Marcia. *Peter Piper's Alphabet*. Scribner's, 1959.

Duvoisin, Roger. *Petunia the Silly Goose Stories*. Knopf, 1987.

GOALS

The children will
▶ develop phonemic awareness.
▶ identify words with the \kw\ blend.
▶ associate \kw\ with the letters **qu.**
▶ engage in interactive writing.
▶ engage in personal writing.
▶ use invented spellings.

MATERIALS

Program materials you will need: student edition pages 100–105, *Assess and Plan File,* BLM 17-Corn

Optional program materials: BLM 17-Talking Ducks

Other optional materials: old magazines, scissors, glue

PERIOD 1

Getting Ready to Teach

▶ Copy the poem from page T101 on chart paper.
▶ Cut the kernels of corn from BLM 17-Corn.

Sharing the Poem (pp. 100–101)

▶ Help the children find pages 100 and 101.
▶ Read the poem to the class, pointing to the words as you read.
▶ Solicit personal responses to the poem. Use these responses and the illustration to guide a brief discussion of the poem.

 **PHONEMIC AWARENESS**

▶ Ask the children to say the word **quack** with you. Then ask them to say \kw\. Ask if anyone has a name that begins like **quack**. (Possible responses: Quincy, Quentin)

▶ Read the poem again. Invite the children to raise their hands each time they hear a word that begins like **quack**.

▶ Explain to the children that they can feed the ducks by completing words. Tell them you will say the last part of a word and you would like them to say the whole word by adding \kw\ at the beginning. Use these word parts: **ick** (**quick**), **een** (**queen**), **iet** (**quiet**), **ilt** (**quilt**), **art** (**quart**), **it** (**quit**), **estion** (**question**), **arter** (**quarter**), **artet** (**quartet**). For each response, display a kernel of corn.

YOUR CHOICE:

SPELLING PLUS

▶ Share the following riddles with the children:
Q. What do ducks like for a snack?
A. Quackers and milk
Q. What happens to ducks that fly upside down?
A. They quack up.

ASSESS AND **PLAN** p. Z19

Quack, Quack!

We have two ducks. One blue. One black.
And when our blue duck goes "Quack-quack"
  our black duck quickly quack-quacks back.
The quacks Blue quacks make her quite a quacker
  but Black is a quicker quacker-backer.

—Dr. Seuss

100   Unit 17   Unit 17   101

Quack, Quack!

We have two ducks. One blue. One black.
And when our blue duck goes "Quack-quack"
  our black duck quickly quack-quacks back.
The quacks Blue quacks make her quite a quacker
  but Black is a quicker quacker-backer.

—Dr. Seuss

 **SOUND-SYMBOL AWARENESS**
(pp. 102–103)

▶ Reread "Quack, Quack!" to the class.

▶ Write capital **Q** and lowercase **q** on a wall chart. Identify the letter and tell the children it is the beginning letter in **quack**.

▶ Help the children find pages 102 and 103. Ask them if they can find a queen in the picture. Write **queen** under **Qq** on the chart. Ask them what letter begins the word **queen**. (Response: **q**)

▶ Ask the children to find other things in the picture whose names start with the same sound as **quack** and **queen**.

FYI ▶ Pictured words are listed at the bottom of the reduced student page.

▶ If you wish to control the naming of the pictured words, ask, *"Do you see a quilt?"* and continue in this manner for each pictured word. If you want the children to initiate the naming of the pictures, provide prompts only as necessary.

▶ Write each word on the chart; say the word, emphasizing the beginning sound; and ask the children to repeat it. Ask what letter begins the word.

▶ Ask the children to notice the second letter in each word you wrote. Tell them this is the letter **u**. Tell them the letter **q** is always followed by **u** in English words. Tell them that together **q** and **u** stand for \kw\.

▶ Ask the children to generate other words that begin like **quack**. Provide prompts and wait time as needed. Add the children's responses to the wall chart.

102   Unit 17

Pictured Words
quilt, queen, quarter, quail, question, quills

 ASSESS AND **PLAN**   p. Z19

USING THE PICTURE-SORT CARDS

After the illustrations on pages 102 and 103 have been identified and discussed, consider using the *Picture-Sort Cards* for this unit. Possible activities include the following:

▶ Duplicate the *Picture-Sort Cards* for this unit and separate them. Distribute one set of cards to individuals or small groups. Say each pictured word aloud. Ask each student to place the pointer finger of his/her right hand on a *Picture-Sort Card* and then to place the pointer finger of his/her left hand on the matching picture in the illustration in their book. (Students working in groups can take turns.) Walk around to provide assistance and praise their efforts. Encourage children to talk about the pictures.

▶ Separate the *Picture-Sort Cards* and place them in an envelope in an activity center. Label the envelope with the targeted letter, e.g., **Q**. Work with individuals or small groups to match each *Picture-Sort Card* with its corresponding picture in the illustration.

For more information on using *Picture-Sort Cards,* see the *Picture-Sort Card Book.*

Unit 17 **103**

YOUR CHOICE:

SPELLING PLUS

▶ Help the children find page 165.

▶ Ask them to find the letters **Qq**. Encourage them to draw a picture of something whose name begins with **q**, or provide old magazines from which they can cut appropriate pictures to glue beside the letters.

▶ You may wish to review words on the wall chart and suggest the children choose one of these to illustrate.

HELPING STUDENTS ACQUIRING ENGLISH

Keep in mind that in Spanish, **qu** is pronounced like the letter **k**. Unlike in English, the **u** following the **q** is silent. This spelling for the \k\ sound occurs before an **i** or an **e**. Before **a, o,** and **u,** \k\ is written with a **c**.

Be sure that Spanish-speaking students pronounce the \w\ sound that is part of the sound represented by the **qu** spelling in English. In Spanish, an equivalent spelling of the \qu\ sound in English would be **cu + vowel**. Write several Spanish words that begin with **cu + vowel** on the chalkboard. Examples include **cuidado (care, caution); cuidadora (caretaker, babysitter); cuando (when); cuesta (hill);** and **cuota (quota).** Then write two or three of the words pictured on pages 102 and 103. Pronounce the Spanish words, followed by the English words, pointing out the similarity in the initial sounds. Be certain that students understand you are not translating, merely pointing out how the spelling of the similar sound differs.

Diversity in Language and Culture

The letter **q** is almost always followed by **u**; the **qu** blend is pronounced \kw\. While not all languages have this blend, it is fairly easy to produce because the tongue is placed in the same position for both \k\ and \w\.

The \k\ sound belongs to the class of consonants known as stops because the air is completely stopped as air pressure builds up in the mouth, and then the blockage is released suddenly, producing a sound. For \k\, the back of the tongue rises and blocks the air at the soft palate, or velum, of the roof of the mouth; \k\ is therefore called a velar stop.

Its closest related sound is \g\, which is like \k\ except that the vocal cords vibrate while the air is being released to produce \g\, while \k\ is voiceless. Babies begin to produce \k\ and \g\ early, and the children in your class will probably not have trouble with these sounds.

For \w\, which follows \k\ in **qu** blends, the tongue remains in the same position. Because \w\ requires the lips to be rounded or pursed, the lips are usually rounded for the entire \kw\ blend. Some children may have a bit of trouble pronouncing this blend, so carefully model it for them.

PERIOD 3

 TEMPORARY SPELLING

(p. 104)

▶ Direct the children's attention to the letter forms at the top of the page.

▶ Demonstrate the formation of capital **Q** and lowercase **q**.

▶ Encourage the children to use this page in one of the following ways:

- to practice writing the letter forms;
- to draw one or more pictures of things whose names begin like **quack** and to label each picture;
- to write words that begin with **q**.

▶ Circulate to observe the children's efforts. Ask them to tell you about their drawing and writing.

▶ Accept temporary spellings.

YOUR CHOICE:

 **SPELLING PLUS**

▶ Invite the children to practice forming **Q** and **q** using tactile media of their choice, such as building blocks or bricks, clay, glitter, straws, or string.

 ASSESS AND **PLAN**　　p. Z19

Letters and Words

Q q

 ASSESS AND **PLAN**　　p. Z19

PERIOD 4

INTERACTIVE WRITING

▶ Reread "Quack, Quack!" aloud.

▶ Ask the children to recall how many ducks were in the poem and what colors they were. Invite them to tell something about each of the ducks in turn.

▶ Write their responses on chart paper in sentence form. As you write, you may wish to invite the children to tell you the initial letter for words that begin with previously introduced sound-letter relationships (**a** through **q**). (Use your judgment to decide whether this activity is developmentally appropriate for your class at this time.)

YOUR CHOICE:

PERSONAL WRITING

▶ Discuss the ways in which ducks are different from children: Ducks have wings, children have arms; ducks have webbed feet, children have toes; ducks have bills, children have lips; and so on.

▶ Ask the children to think about which part of a duck they would like to exchange for a part of themselves. Invite them to draw a self-portrait showing the borrowed duck part.

▶ Encourage them to write about how their life would be different with a duck part.

▶ Encourage temporary spellings.

▶ Allow time for sharing.

My Writing

Emergent Spelling Notes

These two samples show that phonetic spellers represent all the surface sound features in words.

tuth FAre wn hit I wsh mi BeD AND the tuth FAre cam.

DeArGrAMOE.
IM bOS You
TOTALic.TheWITR
HKSWOM.
LOVELeslie

Unit 17   **(105)**

PERSONAL WRITING p. 105

▶ Help the children find page 105.

▶ Choose one of the *Personal Writing Activities* (A–D) listed at the bottom of this page or offer the children a choice.

▶ Accept scribblings, random letters, and invented spellings.

▶ Allow time for the children to share their pictures and writing.

YOUR CHOICE: Review

▶ Use the third and fourth pages of Units 1–16 to review sound-letter relationships. Encourage the children to find the items in each picture whose names begin with the letter shown at the top of the left-hand page.

▶ Pronounce words beginning with the sound-letter relationships you wish to review. Ask the children to name the letter that stands for the beginning sound. Use these words: **dive, nurse, boot, panda, foot, body, coat, ever, inch, gorilla, kiss, hello, ask, copy, ostrich, dance, jungle, fun, lamb, good, help, monkey.**

ASSESS AND PLAN   p. Z19

ADDITIONAL LITERATURE

Elting, Mary, and Michael Folsom. *Q Is for Duck: An Alphabet Guessing Game.* Houghton Mifflin, 1980.

Johnston, Tony. *The Quilt Story.* G.P. Putnam's Sons, 1985.

Stehr, Frederic. *Quack-Quack.* Farrar, Straus & Giroux, 1988.

PERSONAL WRITING ACTIVITIES

Activity A

▶ Distribute BLM 17-Talking Ducks.

▶ Ask the children to imagine a conversation between Blue and Black and to write what they are saying in the balloons above their heads.

Activity B

▶ Help the children draw a large question mark on page 105.

▶ Ask them to draw a picture of something they wonder about.

▶ Encourage them to write a question under the picture.

Activity C

▶ Ask the children to draw pictures of things they can buy for a quarter.

▶ Encourage them to label the pictures or write something about them.

Activity D

▶ Ask the children to draw a crown for a queen.

▶ Encourage them to write a story about the crown or the queen who will wear it.

The children will

▶ develop phonemic awareness.

▶ identify words with the \r\ sound.

▶ associate \r\ with the letter **r**.

▶ engage in interactive writing.

▶ engage in personal writing.

▶ use invented spellings.

M A T E R I A L S

Program materials you will need: student edition pages 106–111, *Assess and Plan File,* BLM 18-Raincoat

Optional program materials: BLMs 18-Calendar and 18-Weather Symbols

Other optional materials: old magazines, scissors, glue, rice or red yarn

P E R I O D 1

Getting Ready to Teach

▶ Copy the poem from page T107 on chart paper.

▶ Cut out the pieces of the raincoat on BLM 18-Raincoat.

Sharing the Poem (pp. 106–107)

▶ Help the children find pages 106 and 107.

▶ Read the poem to the class, pointing to the words as you read.

▶ Solicit personal responses to the poem. Use these responses and the illustration to guide a brief discussion of the poem.

))))))) PHONEMIC AWARENESS

▶ Ask the children to say the word **rain** with you. Ask them what sound they hear at the beginning of **rain**. (Response: \r\) Ask if anyone has a name that begins with this sound. (Possible responses: Rachel, Rosita, Raul, Richard)

▶ Read the poem again. Invite the children to raise their hands each time they hear a word that begins with the same sound as **rain**.

▶ Display the pieces of the puzzle from BLM 18-Raincoat.

▶ Tell the children they can help you make something to keep off the rain by naming words that begin with the same sound as **rain**. For each response, put another piece of the raincoat puzzle in place.

◢ ASSESS AND PLAN   p. Z19

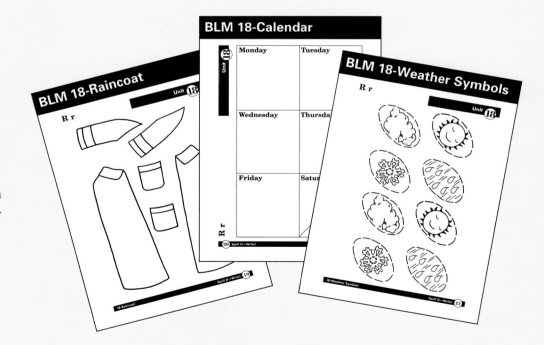

Rainy Day

I do not like a rainy day.

The road is wet, the sky is gray.

They dress me up, from head to toes,

In lots and lots of rubber clothes.

I wish the sun would come and stay.

I do not like a rainy day.

—William Wise

SOUND-SYMBOL AWARENESS
(pp. 108–109)

▶ Reread "Rainy Day" to the class.

▶ Write capital **R** and lowercase **r** on a wall chart. Identify the letter and tell the children it stands for the sound they hear at the beginning of **rain**.

▶ Ask the children to repeat after you first the sound and then the letter several times: \r\, **r**.

▶ Help the children find pages 108 and 109. Ask them if they can find a rabbit in the picture. Write **rabbit** under **Rr** on the chart. Ask them what letter begins the word **rabbit**. (Response: **r**)

▶ Ask the children to find other things in the picture whose names start with the same sound as **rain** and **rabbit**.

FYI Pictured words are listed at the bottom of the reduced student page.

▶ If you wish to control the naming of the pictured words, ask, *"Do you see a rose?"* and continue in this manner for each pictured word. If you want the children to initiate the naming of the pictures, provide prompts only as necessary.

▶ Write each word on the chart; say the word, emphasizing the beginning sound; and ask the children to repeat it. Ask what letter begins the word.

▶ Ask the children to generate other words that begin with the same sound as **rain** and **rabbit**. Provide prompts and wait time as needed. Add the children's responses to the wall chart.

 ASSESS AND **PLAN**　　p. Z19

Pictured Words
robin, rhinoceros, rose, raccoon, ring, rabbit, ribbon, rainbow, rope, rocket, roof

USING THE PICTURE-SORT CARDS

After the illustrations on pages 108 and 109 have been identified and discussed, consider using the *Picture-Sort Cards* for this unit. Possible activities include the following:

▶ Duplicate the *Picture-Sort Cards* for this unit and separate them. Distribute one set of cards to individuals or small groups. Say each pictured word aloud. Ask each student to place the pointer finger of his/her right hand on a *Picture-Sort Card* and then to place the pointer finger of his/her left hand on the matching picture in the illustration in their book. (Students working in groups can take turns.) Walk around to provide assistance and praise their efforts. Encourage children to talk about the pictures.

▶ Separate the *Picture-Sort Cards* and place them in an envelope in an activity center. Label the envelope with the targeted letter, e.g., **R**. Work with individuals or small groups to match each *Picture-Sort Card* with its corresponding picture in the illustration.

For more information on using *Picture-Sort Cards,* see the *Picture-Sort Card Book.*

YOUR CHOICE:

 **SPELLING PLUS**

▶ Help the children find page 166.

▶ Ask them to find the letters **Rr.** Encourage them to draw a picture of something whose name begins with **r,** or provide old magazines from which they can cut appropriate pictures to glue beside the letters.

▶ You may wish to review words on the wall chart and suggest the children choose one of these to illustrate.

YOUR CHOICE:

 SPELLING PLUS

▶ Use BLMs 18-Calendar and 18-Weather Symbols to keep track of the weather for a week. At the end of each day ask the children to help you choose one or more weather symbols to match that day's weather. Display the calendar and affix the appropriate symbols.

FYI This activity may be repeated as often as you like. You may also distribute calendars and symbols to the children and allow them to keep their own records.

Diversity in Language and Culture

The letter **r** stands for a sound that is difficult for many young children to make and equally difficult for linguists to describe. For most American English speakers, \r\ is made by turning the tip of the tongue upward without touching the roof of the mouth. This sound can also be made by bunching the tongue toward the back of the roof of the mouth and keeping the tip of the tongue low. Because the tongue bends back to produce this sound, it is usually called a retroflex **r**.

Many sounds are represented by **r** in languages around the world, including tongue flaps and trills, as in Spanish **pero** (**but**) and **perro** (**dog**).

Some languages do not distinguish between \l\ and \r\. In Japanese and Korean, whether a sound is \r\-like or \l\-like depends on its position in a word or syllable. When such speakers are learning English, they may be confused by the difference between the sounds represented by **l** and **r**.

Many speakers of English, including most British, Australian, South African, and East Coast American English speakers, don't pronounce \r\ after a vowel in such words as **car** and **start,** so that **court** sounds like **caught**.

At first, children may substitute other sounds for \r\. Especially common is \w\—\wed\ for **red,** for example. In time, they will learn to make this sound accurately.

HELPING STUDENTS ACQUIRING ENGLISH

Special pronunciation practice may be needed for students attempting to pronounce the English \r\ sound. (Be sure to take into account the information regarding this sound in this unit's *Diversity in Language and Culture* on this teacher page.)

Ask each student and his or her study buddy to practice the \r\ sound intensely. Ask the English-speaking student to model \r\ using the words pictured on pages 108 and 109 many times until his or her buddy who is acquiring English is able to pronounce them. You may wish to give special attention to any students who find it especially difficult to produce this sound.

TEMPORARY SPELLING

(p. 110)

▶ Direct the children's attention to the letter forms at the top of the page.

▶ Demonstrate the formation of capital **R** and lowercase **r**.

▶ Encourage the children to use this page in one of the following ways:

- to practice writing the letter forms;

- to draw one or more pictures of things whose names begin with the same sound as **rain** and to label each picture;

- to write words that begin with **r**.

▶ Circulate to observe the children's efforts. Ask them to tell you about their drawing and writing.

▶ Accept temporary spellings.

YOUR CHOICE:

 SPELLING PLUS

▶ Invite the children to practice forming **R** and **r** using rice or red yarn. Demonstrate the activity.

 ASSESS AND **PLAN**   p. Z19

Letters and Words

Rr

PERIOD 4

INTERACTIVE WRITING

▶ Reread "Rainy Day" aloud.

▶ Ask the children to recall what the author said about a rainy day and why he does not like it.

▶ Write their responses on chart paper in sentence form. As you write, you may wish to invite the children to tell you the initial letter for words that begin with previously introduced sound-letter relationships (**a** through **r**). (Use your judgment to decide whether this activity is developmentally appropriate for your class at this time.)

YOUR CHOICE:

PERSONAL WRITING

▶ Remind the children that the author of "Rainy Day" says he must wear lots of rubber clothes when it rains.

▶ Invite the children to draw pictures of other types of rain gear.

▶ Encourage them to label their drawings or write something they like or don't like about rainy days.

▶ Encourage temporary spellings.

▶ Allow time for sharing.

 ASSESS AND **PLAN**   p. Z19

My Writing

Emergent Spelling Notes

This story by Dan makes use of phonetic spelling. When children invent spellings, they are *thinking* about spelling.

the shrff olwaz chass the Dukes.
the Dukes get away.
they have a cat named the Ginrl Lie

Unit 18 (111)

PERIOD 5

PERSONAL WRITING p. 111

▶ Help the children find page 111.

▶ Choose one of the *Personal Writing Activities* (A–D) listed at the bottom of this page or offer the children a choice.

▶ Accept scribblings, random letters, and invented spellings.

▶ Allow time for the children to share their pictures and writing.

ASSESS AND PLAN p. Z19

PERSONAL WRITING ACTIVITIES

Activity A

▶ Discuss recess with the children. Invite them to draw a picture of what they like to do during recess.

▶ Encourage them to write something that tells about the picture.

Activity B

▶ Talk with the children about the color red and things that might be red— apples, flowers, hair, fire trucks, traffic lights, stop signs, and so on.

▶ Invite the children to draw or cut from magazines pictures of things that are red.

▶ Encourage them to label their drawings or write something about them.

Activity C

▶ Invite the children to imagine that their kitchen at home is a restaurant. Ask them to make a list of the foods most often served in this "restaurant."

▶ Suggest they illustrate their lists.

Activity D

▶ Write **rabbit, raccoon, reindeer,** and **robin** on the chalkboard.

▶ Invite the children to write a story about one or more of these animals.

▶ Encourage them to give their animals names that begin with **R** and to illustrate their writing.

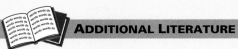

ADDITIONAL LITERATURE

Hutchins, Pat. *The Doorbell Rang.* Greenwillow Books, 1986.

Jonas, Ann. *Round Trip.* Greenwillow Books, 1983.

Kalan, Robert. *Rain.* Greenwillow Books, 1978.

Marshall, James. *Red Riding Hood.* Dial Books for Young Readers, 1988.

Peek, Merle. *Roll Over! A Counting Song.* Houghton Mifflin, 1981.

Scheer, Julian. *Rain Makes Applesauce.* Holiday House, 1964.

G O A L S

The children will

▶ develop phonemic awareness.

▶ identify words with the \s\ sound.

▶ associate \s\ with the letter **s**.

▶ engage in interactive writing.

▶ engage in personal writing.

▶ use invented spellings.

M A T E R I A L S

Program materials you will need: student edition pages 112–117, *Assess and Plan File,* BLMs 19-Pie and 19-Blackbirds

Optional materials: old magazines, scissors, glue, sandpaper, seeds (marigold, sunflower, or pumpkin)

P E R I O D 1

Getting Ready to Teach

▶ Copy the poem from page T113 on chart paper.

Sharing the Poem (pp. 112–113)

▶ Help the children find pages 112 and 113.

▶ Read the poem to the class, pointing to the words as you read.

▶ Solicit personal responses to the poem. Use these responses and the illustration to guide a brief discussion of the poem.

▶ Invite the class to sing or chant the poem with you.

))))))))))) PHONEMIC AWARENESS

▶ Ask the children to say the word **sing** with you. Ask them what sound they hear at the beginning of **sing**. (Response: **s**) Ask if anyone has a name that begins with this sound. (Possible responses: Sam, Simon, Sara, Susan)

▶ Read the poem again. Invite the children to raise their hands each time they hear a word that begins with the same sound as **sing**.

▶ Encourage the children to look around the classroom for objects whose names begin like **sing**. (Possible responses: sack, seats, signs, sink, soap, socks)

▶ Tell the children they can make new words by adding \s\ to the beginning of words you say. Demonstrate by saying "**add, sad**" and asking the children to repeat the words. Use these words: **Ed** (**said**), **ail** (**sail**), **and** (**sand**), **alley** (**Sally**), **aim** (**same**), **at** (**sat**), **elf** (**self**), **end** (**send**), **oh** (**so**), **it** (**sit**), **ink** (**sink**), **I** (**sigh**).

◣ **ASSESS** AND **PLAN**   p. Z19

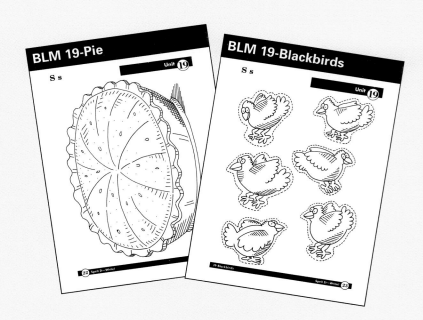

Sing a Song of Sixpence

Sing a song of sixpence,
  a pocket full of rye;
Four-and-twenty blackbirds
  baked in a pie!
When the pie was opened
  the birds began to sing;
Wasn't that a dainty dish
  to set before the King?

Getting Ready to Teach

▶ Cut out the pie on BLM 19-Pie. Cut 24 blackbirds using BLM 19-Blackbirds as a pattern. Tack the bottom and sides of the pie to a bulletin board to form a pocket and place the blackbirds inside.

ABC)) SOUND-SYMBOL AWARENESS
(pp. 114–115)

▶ Reread "Sing a Song of Sixpence" to the class.

▶ Write capital **S** and lowercase **s** on a wall chart. Identify the letter and tell the children it stands for the sound they hear at the beginning of **sing**.

▶ Ask the children to repeat after you first the sound and then the letter several times: \s\, **s**.

▶ Help the children find pages 114 and 115. Ask them if they can find a sandwich in the picture. Write **sandwich** under **Ss** on the chart. Ask them what letter begins the word **sandwich**. (Response: **s**)

▶ Ask the children to find other things in the picture whose names start with the same sound as **sing** and **sandwich**.

FYI Pictured words are listed at the bottom of the reduced student page.

▶ If you wish to control the naming of the pictured words, ask, *"Do you see a seal?"* and continue in this manner for each pictured word. If you want the children to initiate the naming of the pictures, provide prompts only as necessary.

▶ Write each word on the chart; say the word, emphasizing the beginning sound; and ask the children to repeat it. Ask what letter begins the word.

▶ Ask the children to generate other words that begin with the same sound as **sing**. Tell them that for each answer a blackbird will fly out of the pie. (For each response, remove a blackbird from the pie pocket and tack it elsewhere on the bulletin board.) Provide prompts and wait time as needed. Add the children's responses to the wall chart.

FYI If children name words that begin with **c**, write these words on the wall chart in a separate column and explain that sometimes \s\ is spelled **c**.

◤ ASSESS AND PLAN   p. Z19

Ss

SOAP

114   Unit 19

Pictured Words
seven, sandwich, seal, saw, soap, socks, sun, suspenders, saddle, soup

USING THE PICTURE-SORT CARDS

After the illustrations on pages 114 and 115 have been identified and discussed, consider using the *Picture-Sort Cards* for this unit. Possible activities include the following:

▶ Duplicate the *Picture-Sort Cards* for this unit and separate them. Distribute one set of cards to individuals or small groups. Say each pictured word aloud. Ask each student to place the pointer finger of his/her right hand on a *Picture-Sort Card* and then to place the pointer finger of his/her left hand on the matching picture in the illustration in their book. (Students working in

groups can take turns.) Walk around to provide assistance and praise their efforts. Encourage children to talk about the pictures.

▶ Separate the *Picture-Sort Cards* and place them in an envelope in an activity center. Label the envelope with the targeted letter, e.g., **S**. Work with individuals or small groups to match each *Picture-Sort Card* with its corresponding picture in the illustration.

For more information on using *Picture-Sort Cards,* see the *Picture-Sort Card Book.*

Unit 19 **115**

YOUR CHOICE:

SPELLING PLUS

▶ Help the children find page 166.

▶ Ask them to find the letters **Ss**. Encourage them to draw a picture of something whose name begins with **s,** or provide old magazines from which they can cut appropriate pictures to glue beside the letters.

▶ You may wish to review words on the wall chart and suggest the children choose one of these to illustrate.

Diversity in Language and Culture

The \s\ sound may be represented by **s,** by **c,** and by several combinations of letters. This unit focuses on \s\ spelled **s.**

The \s\ sound belongs to a class of consonant sounds called fricatives. A fricative forces air through a narrow path to create a sound. Fricatives in English include \f\, \th\, and \sh\.

The \s\ sound involves curling the sides of the tongue slightly and bringing the flat part of the tongue up toward the back of the upper front teeth. Air is then forced through the rounded space.

The closest sound to \s\ is \z\, which is produced in the same way as \s\ except that the vocal cords are

vibrating as \z\ is produced. If you try to whisper a word with \z\ (like **zebra**), you will hear a voiceless \s\ instead. Some languages, such as Spanish, have only voiceless \s\ and lack a true \z\, as it is pronounced in English, altogether.

Hawaiian has no \s\ or \z\. In some other languages, such as Japanese, \s\ becomes \sh\ before some vowels. Japanese learners of English might pronounce a word such as **season** as **sheed-zun**\.

If children in your class lisp or have trouble producing \s\, model the sound carefully. In most cases, the problem will disappear in time.

HELPING STUDENTS ACQUIRING ENGLISH

Ask Spanish-speaking students to identify as many words as possible in the illustrations on pages 114 and 115 that also begin with the \s\ sound in Spanish. Students should identify: **silla (saddle)**; **siete (seven)**; **sandwich (sandwich)**; **sopa (soup)**; **sierra (saw)**; **sol (sun)**.

Call attention to the different pronunciations of s at the end of **socks** (\s\) and at the end of **suspenders** (\z\). Spanish does not pronounce s as \z\. Ask students to contrast these words, pronouncing them several times.

TEMPORARY SPELLING

(p. 116)

▶ Direct the children's attention to the letter forms at the top of the page.

▶ Demonstrate the formation of capital **S** and lowercase **s**.

▶ Encourage the children to use this page in one of the following ways:

- to practice writing the letter forms;

- to draw one or more pictures of things whose names begin with the same sound as **sing** and to label each picture;

- to write words that begin with **s**.

▶ Circulate to observe the children's efforts. Ask them to tell you about their drawing and writing.

▶ Accept temporary spellings.

YOUR CHOICE:

 SPELLING PLUS

▶ Invite the children to practice forming **S** and **s** by having them cut the letters from fine sandpaper and trace over them with a finger. Demonstrate the activity.

◤ **ASSESS** AND **PLAN**   p. Z19

 **Letters and Words**

S s

PERIOD 4

✎ **INTERACTIVE WRITING**

▶ Reread "Sing a Song of Sixpence" aloud.

▶ Ask the children what they think the king might have said when the birds began to sing.

▶ Write their responses on chart paper in sentence form. As you write, you may wish to invite the children to tell you the initial letter for words that begin with previously introduced sound-letter relationships (**a** through **s**). (Use your judgment to decide whether this activity is developmentally appropriate for your class at this time.)

YOUR CHOICE:

✎ **PERSONAL WRITING**

▶ Ask the children to think about a song they like to sing.

▶ Encourage them to write the title and as many of the words as they can remember. Suggest they illustrate their songs.

▶ Encourage temporary spellings.

▶ Allow time for sharing.

◤ **ASSESS** AND **PLAN**   p. Z19

My Writing

Emergent Spelling Notes

Writing stories using invented spelling helps set the foundations for later spelling competency. This story by Dan includes phonetic spelling.

My oll truck

My truck is gray.
My truck shuts water out. on the side it ses Mobol. It rols and jumps ramps,
It's black, blue, red and white. I play weth it.

PERSONAL WRITING   p. 117

▶ Help the children find page 117.

▶ Choose one of the *Personal Writing Activities* (A–D) listed at the bottom of this page or offer the children a choice.

▶ Accept scribblings, random letters, and invented spellings.

▶ Allow time for the children to share their pictures and writing.

ASSESS AND PLAN   p. Z19

PERSONAL WRITING ACTIVITIES

Activity A

▶ Write *A Super Sandwich* on the chalkboard. Read the words and ask the children to copy the title on page 117.

▶ Invite the children to draw a picture of their favorite sandwich.

▶ Encourage them to list the ingredients and any special tips for making the sandwich.

Activity B

▶ Write *Surprise!* on the chalkboard. Read the word and ask the children to copy it at the top of page 117.

▶ Invite the children to write a story with this title or to draw a picture of a surprise they would like to have and write something about it.

Activity C

▶ Distribute seeds, such as marigold, sunflower, or pumpkin seeds. Ask the children to glue a seed on page 117.

▶ Invite them to draw a picture to show what might sprout from the seed. Tell them it may be a real or an imaginary plant.

▶ Encourage them to give the plant a name or write something about it.

Activity D

▶ Invite the children to think of a story title that has at least two words that start with s.

▶ Encourage them to work with one or two partners to write a story for the title.

▶ Invite them to illustrate their writing.

ADDITIONAL LITERATURE

de Regniers, Beatrice Schenk, Eva Moore, Mary Michaels White, and Jan Carr, compilers. *Sing a Song of Popcorn: Every Child's Book of Poems.* Scholastic, 1988.

Emberley, Barbara. *Simon's Song.* Prentice-Hall, 1969.

Root, Phyllis. *Soup for Supper.* Harper & Row, 1986.

Simon, Seymour. *Soap Bubble Magic.* Lothrop, 1985.

Ziefert, Harriet. *So Sick!* Random House, 1985.

G O A L S

The children will

▶ develop phonemic awareness.

▶ identify words with the \t\ sound.

▶ associate \t\ with the letter **t.**

▶ engage in interactive writing.

▶ engage in personal writing.

▶ use invented spellings.

M A T E R I A L S

Program materials you will need: student edition pages 118–123, *Assess and Plan File,* BLM 20-Tadpoles and Frogs

Optional materials: old magazines, scissors, glue, tinsel, pictures of tigers

P E R I O D 1

Getting Ready to Teach

▶ Copy the poem from page T119 on chart paper.

▶ Make at least three copies of BLM 20-Tadpoles and Frogs. Cut out 15 or more tadpoles and frogs.

Sharing the Poem (pp. 118–119)

▶ Help the children find pages 118 and 119.

▶ Read the poem to the class, pointing to the words as you read.

▶ Solicit personal responses to the poem. Use these responses and the illustration to guide a brief discussion of the poem.

▶ Explain and demonstrate the following movements to go with the lines of the poem:

• Line 1: Rub your eyes as if you were crying.

• Line 2: Look behind you as if you were looking for your tail.

• Line 3: Shake your head and your index finger.

• Line 4: Crouch down and jump like a frog.

▶ Invite the children to recite the poem with you and use these actions to dramatize it.

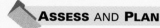
PHONEMIC AWARENESS

▶ Ask the children to say the word **tadpole** with you. Ask them what sound they hear at the beginning of **tadpole.** (Response: \t\) Ask if anyone has a name that begins with this sound. (Possible responses: Teresa, Tien, Ted, Tom)

▶ Read the poem again. Invite the children to raise their hands each time they hear a word that begins with the same sound as **tadpole.**

▶ Encourage the children to look around the classroom for objects whose names begin like **tadpole.** (Possible responses: tables, tacks, tape, teacher, teeth, telephone, tongues, towels, toys)

▶ Draw a pond on the chalkboard. Attach the tadpoles inside the pond. Set the frogs aside.

▶ Say **tadpole.** Ask these questions:

• Do you hear \t\? (Response: yes)

• Do you hear \t\ at the beginning or the end of **tadpole**? (Response: at the beginning)

▶ Say **boat.** Ask these questions:

• Do you hear \t\? (Response: yes)

• Do you hear \t\ at the beginning or the end of **boat**? (Response: at the end)

▶ If the children have trouble hearing \t\ at the end of **boat,** pronounce several other words ending with \t\. Emphasize final \t\ as you say the following words and ask the children to listen for \t\ at the end of each word: **cat, hat, coat, bought, write.**

▶ Tell the children they can change tadpoles into frogs by saying whether a word begins or ends with \t\.

▶ Pronounce words that begin or end with \t\. Ask the children to say "beginning" if they hear \t\ at the beginning and to say "end" if they hear \t\ at the end.

▶ For each correct response, remove a tadpole from the pond and replace it with a frog, saying "Ribbit."

▶ Use these words: **pat, tap, tip, pit, tail, late, top, pot, tube, boot, tight.** (For **tight,** the children should answer "beginning and end.")

◤ **ASSESS** AND **PLAN**   p. Z19

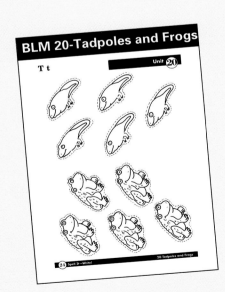

Growing Up

Little Tommy Tadpole began to weep and wail,
For little Tommy Tadpole had lost his little tail,
And his mother didn't know him, as he wept upon a log;
For he wasn't Tommy Tadpole, but Mr. Thomas Frog.

—C.J. Dennis

Growing Up

Little Tommy Tadpole began to weep and wail,
For little Tommy Tadpole had lost his little tail,
And his mother didn't know him, as he wept upon a log;
For he wasn't Tommy Tadpole, but Mr. Thomas Frog.

—C.J. Dennis

SOUND-SYMBOL AWARENESS
(pp. 120–121)

▶ Reread "Growing Up" to the class.

▶ Write capital **T** and lowercase **t** on a wall chart. Identify the letter and tell the children it stands for the sound they hear at the beginning of **tadpole**.

▶ Ask the children to repeat after you first the sound and then the letter several times: \t\, **t**.

▶ Help the children find pages 120 and 121. Ask them if they can find a tadpole in the picture. Write **tadpole** under **Tt** on the chart. Ask them what letter begins the word **tadpole**. (Response: **t**)

▶ Ask the children to find other things in the picture whose names start with the same sound as **tadpole**.

FYI ▷ Pictured words are listed at the bottom of the reduced student page.

▶ If you wish to control the naming of the pictured words, ask, *"Do you see a turtle?"* and continue in this manner for each pictured word. If you want the children to initiate the naming of the pictures, provide prompts only as necessary.

▶ Write each word on the chart; say the word, emphasizing the beginning sound; and ask the children to repeat it. Ask what letter begins the word.

▶ Ask the children to generate other words that begin with the same sound as **tadpole**. Provide prompts and wait time as needed. Add the children's responses to the wall chart.

 ASSESS AND **PLAN**   p. Z19

120   Unit 20

Pictured Words
tadpole, towel, tomato, turtle, tent, turkey, table, telephone, ten, tiger, tail, two

USING THE PICTURE-SORT CARDS

After the illustrations on pages 120 and 121 have been identified and discussed, consider using the *Picture-Sort Cards* for this unit. Possible activities include the following:

▶ Duplicate the *Picture-Sort Cards* for this unit and separate them. Distribute one set of cards to individuals or small groups. Say each pictured word aloud. Ask each student to place the pointer finger of his/her right hand on a *Picture-Sort Card* and then to place the pointer finger of his/her left hand on the matching picture in the illustration in their book. (Students working in groups can take turns.) Walk around to provide assistance and praise their efforts. Encourage children to talk about the pictures.

▶ Separate the *Picture-Sort Cards* and place them in an envelope in an activity center. Label the envelope with the targeted letter, e.g., **T**. Work with individuals or small groups to match each *Picture-Sort Card* with its corresponding picture in the illustration.

For more information on using *Picture-Sort Cards,* see the *Picture-Sort Card Book.*

▶ Help the children find page 166.

▶ Ask them to find the letters **Tt**. Encourage them to draw a picture of something whose name begins with **t,** or provide old magazines from which they can cut appropriate pictures to glue beside the letters.

▶ You may wish to review words on the wall chart and suggest the children choose one of these to illustrate.

Diversity in Language and Culture

This unit focuses on the \t\ sound spelled **t**. Like \k\ and \p\, \t\ is a stop: air is completely blocked in the mouth as air pressure builds up and is then released all at once. While \p\ blocks the air at the lips and \k\ blocks the air at the back of the roof of the mouth, \t\ blocks the air with the tip of the tongue against the bony ridge at the back of the teeth. It is thus a dental stop. It is unvoiced, like \p\ and \k\, which means the vocal cords do not start vibrating until after the air is released.

The \t\ sound is common in languages around the world. Related to \t\ is its voiced counterpart, \d\. American English speakers tend to pronounce \t\ and \d\ the same between vowels. The words **ladder** and **latter** sound the same; the consonant sound between the vowels in both words is voiced.

HELPING STUDENTS ACQUIRING ENGLISH

Write a list of the words pictured on pages 120 and 121 on the chalkboard. Ask the students to work with their study buddies to write simple short sentences that use these words and identify what is happening in the picture. Study buddy pairs should be made up of one student who is acquiring English and a student whose primary language is English or who has reached a more advanced stage of English acquisition. (Possible responses: There is a towel on the tent. A boy and a turkey ride the tiger. There is a turtle under the table, etc.)

Then ask the students to try to use as many words from the list as they are able in a single sentence. Remind them to copy the spelling carefully. Check each pair of students to see who came up with the longest sentence. Share the sentence(s) with the class.

TEMPORARY SPELLING

(p. 122)

▶ Direct the children's attention to the letter forms at the top of the page.

▶ Demonstrate the formation of capital **T** and lowercase **t**.

▶ Encourage the children to use this page in one of the following ways:

  • to practice writing the letter forms;

  • to draw one or more pictures of things whose names begin with the same sound as **tadpole** and to label each picture;

  • to write words that begin with **t**.

▶ Circulate to observe the children's efforts. Ask them to tell you about their drawing and writing.

▶ Accept temporary spellings.

YOUR CHOICE:

 SPELLING PLUS

▶ Invite the children to practice forming **T** and **t** using tinsel. Demonstrate the activity.

 ASSESS AND PLAN   **p. Z19**

Letters and Words

T t

PERIOD 4

INTERACTIVE WRITING

▶ Reread "Growing Up" aloud.

▶ Ask the children what happened to Tommy Tadpole in the poem. (Possible responses: He lost his tail. He grew up. He became a frog.)

▶ Write their responses on chart paper in sentence form. As you write, you may wish to invite the children to tell you the initial letter for words that begin with previously introduced sound-letter relationships (**a** through **t**). (Use your judgment to decide whether this activity is developmentally appropriate for your class at this time.)

YOUR CHOICE:

PERSONAL WRITING

▶ Discuss with the children the idea that animals and people change as they grow. Ask them what they are looking forward to about growing up.

▶ Invite them to draw a picture of something they hope to do when they are older.

▶ Encourage them to write something about the picture.

▶ Encourage temporary spellings.

▶ Allow time for sharing.

ASSESS AND PLAN   **p. Z19**

My Writing

Emergent Spelling Notes

This speller is moving out of phonetic into transitional spelling. Transitional spellings in this example include **Lillte, wod's,** and **huose.**

The three **pig's** Lillte one bay a Mut hr. pig Sent. her three Lillte pig's Ot inot The woD's. The Frst Litl pig Met a MaN With a BuN DI u.v. ctRo The pig seD my tAte ctorto Bilb MaN GivM E his

Unit 20 **123**

PERSONAL WRITING p. 123

▶ Help the children find page 123.
▶ Choose one of the *Personal Writing Activities* (A–D) listed at the bottom of this page or offer the children a choice.
▶ Accept scribblings, random letters, and invented spellings.
▶ Allow time for the children to share their pictures and writing.

ASSESS AND PLAN p. Z19

PERSONAL WRITING ACTIVITIES

Activity A

▶ Read *The Teeny-Tiny Woman* to the class. (See *Additional Literature*.)
▶ Invite the children to illustrate their favorite part of the story.
▶ Encourage them to write about why they liked it.

Activity B

▶ Ask the children to write the name of their favorite television show and what it is about.
▶ Invite them to illustrate their writing.

Activity C

▶ Invite the children to draw a picture of their favorite toy and write something about it.

Activity D

▶ Discuss tigers with the children and show some pictures, if possible.
▶ Invite the children to write a story about a real or make-believe tiger and illustrate it.

ADDITIONAL LITERATURE

Burton, Marilee Robin. *Tails Toes Eyes Ears Nose*. Harper & Row, 1989.

Galdone, Paul. *The Teeny-Tiny Woman*. Houghton Mifflin, 1984.

McGovern, Ann. *Too Much Noise*. Houghton Mifflin, 1967.

Mosel, Arlene. *Tikki Tikki Tembo*. Holt, Rinehart & Winston, 1968.

Zolotow, Charlotte. *Timothy Too!* Houghton Mifflin, 1986.

GOALS

The children will

▶ develop phonemic awareness.

▶ identify words with the **short u** sound.

▶ associate the **short u** sound with the letter **u**.

▶ engage in interactive writing.

▶ engage in personal writing.

▶ use invented spellings.

MATERIALS

Program materials you will need: student edition pages 124–129, *Assess and Plan File,* BLM 21-Umbrella

Other materials you will need: a large fresh mushroom

Optional materials: old magazines, scissors, glue, uncooked macaroni

PERIOD 1

Getting Ready to Teach

▶ Copy the poem from page T125 on chart paper.

▶ Cut out the pieces of the umbrella on BLM 21-Umbrella.

Sharing the Poem (pp. 124–125)

▶ Help the children find pages 124 and 125.

▶ Read the poem to the class, pointing to the words as you read.

▶ Solicit personal responses to the poem. Use these responses and the illustration to guide a brief discussion of the poem.

))))) PHONEMIC AWARENESS

▶ Ask the children to say the word **umbrella** with you. Ask them what sound they hear at the beginning of **umbrella**. (Response: \uh\)

▶ Read the poem again. Invite the children to raise their hands each time they hear a word that begins with the same sound as **umbrella**.

▶ Invite the children to help you make an umbrella to keep off the rain. Tell them you will say a word in slow motion and ask them to say it in a normal way. For example, if you say **fun** as \f\-\uh\-\n\, the children should respond "fun." Each time they say a word correctly, position a piece of the umbrella puzzle.

▶ Use words that have a **short u** sound and only two or three phonemes, such as **up, us, bus, run, duck, sun, cut, bug, cup, puff, hum.**

◣ ASSESS AND PLAN   p. Z19

BLM 21-Umbrella

U Is for Umbrellas

U is for Umbrellas
    That bloom in rainy weather,
Like many-colored mushrooms,
    Sprouting upward altogether.
How useful an umbrella is!
    But still I often wonder
If a roof on stormy evenings
    Isn't nicer to be under.

—Phyllis McGinley

U Is for Umbrellas

U is for Umbrellas
    That bloom in rainy weather,
Like many-colored mushrooms,
    Sprouting upward altogether.
How useful an umbrella is!
    But still I often wonder
If a roof on stormy evenings
    Isn't nicer to be under.

—Phyllis McGinley

SOUND-SYMBOL AWARENESS
(pp. 126–127)

▶ Reread "U Is for Umbrellas" to the class.

▶ Write capital **U** and lowercase **u** on a wall chart. Identify the letter and tell the children it stands for the sound they hear at the beginning of **umbrella**.

▶ Ask the children to repeat after you first the sound and then the letter several times: \uh\, **u**.

▶ Help the children find pages 126 and 127. Ask them if they can find an umbrella in the picture. Write **umbrella** under **Uu** on the chart. Ask them what letter begins the word **umbrella**. (Response: **u**)

▶ Ask the children to find other things in the picture whose names start with the same sound as **umbrella**.

FYI Pictured words are listed at the bottom of the reduced student page.

▶ If you wish to control the naming of the pictured words, ask, *"Do you see an undershirt?"* and continue in this manner for each pictured word. If you want the children to initiate the naming of the pictures, provide prompts only as necessary.

▶ Write each word on the chart; say the word, emphasizing the beginning **short u** sound; and ask the children to repeat it. Ask what letter begins the word.

▶ Ask the children to generate other words that begin with the same sound as **umbrella**. Provide prompts and wait time as needed. Add the children's responses to the wall chart.

126 Unit 21

Pictured Words
short u: umbrella, up, undershirt, umpire
long u: ukulele, uniform, unicorn

YOUR CHOICE:

SPELLING PLUS

▶ If you wish to introduce **long u**, write **uniform** on a wall chart. Say the word and ask the children to repeat it. Ask them what sound they hear at the beginning of **uniform**. (Response: \yoo\) Ask what letter begins the word **uniform**. (Response: **u**)

▶ Ask the children if they can find anything in the picture on pages 126 and 127 whose name begins with the same sound as **uniform**. Elicit responses as you did for words beginning with the **short u** sound.

▶ Write each word on the chart; say the word, emphasizing the **long u** sound; and ask the children to repeat it.

▶ Ask the children to generate other words that begin with the same sound as **uniform**. Provide prompts and wait time as needed. Add responses to the wall chart.

ASSESS AND PLAN   p. Z19

USING THE PICTURE-SORT CARDS

After the illustrations on pages 126 and 127 have been identified and discussed, consider using the *Picture-Sort Cards* for this unit. For more information on using *Picture-Sort Cards,* see page T120 or the *Picture-Sort Card Book.*

Unit 2I **127**

▶ Help the children find page 167.

▶ Ask them to find the letters **Uu.** Encourage them to draw a picture of something whose name begins with **u,** or provide old magazines from which they can cut appropriate pictures to glue beside the letters.

▶ You may wish to review words on the wall chart and suggest the children choose one of these to illustrate.

Diversity in Language and Culture

The letter **u** stands for several sounds in English. This unit focuses on **short u,** as in **umbrella,** and makes note of **long u,** as in **uniform.**

The **short u** sound is pronounced with the tongue pushed back and the jaw open midway. This sound is called an unrounded mid-back vowel. (For some speakers, the tongue is not pushed back as far as for other speakers; in this case, the sound is called a mid-central vowel.)

The **long u** sound (combined with an initial \y\ sound) is also a back vowel, but the jaw is not dropped. It is a high back vowel, and the lips are rounded (or pursed together). It is a common vowel sound in languages around the world.

A few languages, including Japanese and Korean, pronounce the **long u** sound with the lips spread rather than rounded. Some learners of English from such language backgrounds transfer this lip position when they try to pronounce the English vowel sound.

HELPING STUDENTS ACQUIRING ENGLISH

In some languages, the pronunciation of vowels is consistent, and the concept of "long" and "short" vowels may not exist. Also, the sounds of certain vowels in English may be unfamiliar to students from other language backgrounds. For example, to Spanish-language students **long u** will sound like a diphthong, **iu,** as in **ciudad** (city). Also, there is no **short u** or \uh\ sound for the letter **u** in Spanish—or for any other letter! Pronounce the \uh\ sound with students several times, then add consonants, e.g., **up, pup, cup.** Repeat each word until the students can pronounce them correctly. Use the same procedure to practice the **long u** sound.

TEMPORARY SPELLING

(p. 128)

▶ Direct the children's attention to the letter forms at the top of the page.

▶ Demonstrate the formation of capital **U** and lowercase **u**.

▶ Encourage the children to use this page in one of the following ways:

- to practice writing the letter forms;

- to draw one or more pictures of things whose names begin with the same sound as **umbrella** and to label each picture;

- to write words that begin with **u**.

▶ Circulate to observe the children's efforts. Ask them to tell you about their drawing and writing.

▶ Accept temporary spellings.

YOUR CHOICE:

 **SPELLING PLUS**

▶ Invite the children to practice forming **U** and **u** using uncooked macaroni. Demonstrate the activity.

◥ **ASSESS** AND **PLAN**   p. Z19

 Letters and Words

U u

PERIOD 4

✎ **INTERACTIVE WRITING**

▶ Reread "U Is for Umbrellas" aloud.

▶ Ask the children to recall what the author says umbrellas are like. (Response: mushrooms) Show a real mushroom for comparison.

▶ Ask the children to suggest other things umbrellas are like.

▶ Write their responses on chart paper in sentence form. As you write, you may wish to invite the children to tell you the initial letter for words that begin with previously introduced sound-letter relationships (**a** through **u**). (Use your judgment to decide whether this activity is developmentally appropriate for your class at this time.)

YOUR CHOICE:

✎ **PERSONAL WRITING**

▶ Ask the children to draw a picture of something they like to do—indoors or outdoors—on a rainy day.

▶ Encourage them to describe the picture in writing.

▶ Encourage temporary spellings.

▶ Allow time for sharing.

◥ **ASSESS** AND **PLAN**   p. Z19

My Writing

Emergent Spelling Notes

Writing stories using invented spelling helps set the foundations for later spelling competency. This story by Steven includes transitional spelling.

> Today were gowing to talk about snaycks. A snayck is a animul that slithers at and can be dayjris and can be puyscnis. Sum ar not. It can sqtwes you if you bot it. Cefl. You can be in dayjre by a snayck.
> the in

Unit 21 **129**

PERIOD 5

PERSONAL WRITING p. 129

▶ Help the children find page 129.

▶ Choose one of the *Personal Writing Activities* (A–D) listed at the bottom of this page or offer the children a choice.

▶ Accept scribblings, random letters, and invented spellings.

▶ Allow time for the children to share their pictures and writing.

ASSESS AND **PLAN**   p. Z19

PERSONAL WRITING ACTIVITIES

Activity A

▶ Ask the children to think of things that go up. (Possible responses: balloons, kites, birds, airplanes, escalators, elevators, smoke, rockets)

▶ Invite them to draw a picture of something that goes up and to label it or write about it.

Activity B

▶ Discuss with the children things that live underground.

▶ Invite them to draw an underground scene.

▶ Encourage them to label their pictures or write something about them.

Activity C

▶ Discuss with the children things that live or move underwater.

▶ Invite them to draw an underwater scene.

▶ Encourage them to label their pictures or write something about them.

Activity D

▶ Invite the children to invent something unusual and useful and to draw a picture of it.

▶ Encourage them to describe the invention in writing.

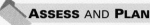

ADDITIONAL LITERATURE

Andersen, Hans Christian (retold by Marianna Mayer). *The Ugly Duckling.* Macmillan, 1987.

Kandoian, Ellen. *Under the Sun.* Dodd, Mead, 1987.

Martin, Bill, Jr., and John Archambault. *Up and Down on the Merry-Go-Round.* Henry Holt, 1988.

G O A L S

The children will

▶ develop phonemic awareness.

▶ identify words with the \v\ sound.

▶ associate \v\ with the letter **v.**

▶ engage in interactive writing.

▶ engage in personal writing.

▶ use invented spellings.

M A T E R I A L S

Program materials you will need: student edition pages 130–135, *Assess and Plan File*

Optional program materials: BLM 22-Valentine

Other optional materials: old magazines, scissors, glue, small valentine hearts or scraps of velvet, clear drinking glass, tablespoon, measuring cup, baking soda, vinegar

P E R I O D 1

Getting Ready to Teach

▶ Copy the poem from page T131 on chart paper.

Sharing the Poem (pp. 130–131)

▶ Help the children find pages 130 and 131.

▶ Read the poem to the class, pointing to the words as you read.

▶ Solicit personal responses to the poem. Use these responses and the illustration to guide a brief discussion of the poem.

 **PHONEMIC AWARENESS**

▶ Ask the children to say the word **valentine** with you. Ask them what sound they hear at the beginning of **valentine.** (Response: \v\) Ask if anyone has a name that begins with this sound. (Possible responses: Victor, Vincent, Virginia, Valerie)

▶ Read the poem again. Invite the children to raise their hands each time they hear a word that begins with the same sound as **valentine.**

▶ Tell the children you will ask them several riddles. Explain that the answer to each riddle is a word that begins or ends with the same sound that begins **valentine.** Use these riddles:

• You can put a flower in this, and it starts with \v\. (**vase**)

• This is the opposite of **hate,** and it ends with \v\. (**love**)

• This is the opposite of **take,** and it ends with \v\. (**give**)

• This is an ice-cream flavor, and it starts with \v\. (**vanilla**)

• This is what you talk with, and it starts with \v\. (**voice**)

• This is a number between one and ten, and it ends with \v\. (**five**)

◢ **ASSESS** AND **PLAN**   p. Z19

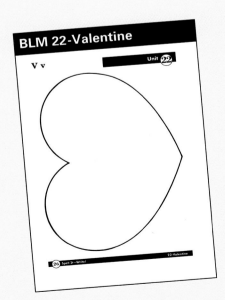

Roses Are Red

Roses are red.
Violets are blue.
Sugar is sweet,
And so are you.

Be my valentine.

SOUND-SYMBOL AWARENESS

(pp. 132–133)

▶ Reread "Roses Are Red" to the class.

▶ Write capital **V** and lowercase **v** on a wall chart. Identify the letter and tell the children it stands for the sound they hear at the beginning of **valentine**.

▶ Ask the children to repeat after you first the sound and then the letter several times: \v\, **v**.

▶ Help the children find pages 132 and 133. Ask them if they can find a valentine in the picture. Write **valentine** under **Vv** on the chart. Ask them what letter begins the word **valentine**. (Response: **v**)

▶ Ask the children to find other things in the picture whose names start with the same sound as **valentine**.

FYI Pictured words are listed at the bottom of the reduced student page.

▶ If you wish to control the naming of the pictured words, ask, *"Do you see a vase?"* and continue in this manner for each pictured word. If you want the children to initiate the naming of the pictures, provide prompts only as necessary.

▶ Write each word on the chart; say the word, emphasizing the beginning sound; and ask the children to repeat it. Ask what letter begins the word.

▶ Ask the children to generate other words that begin with the same sound as **valentine**. Provide prompts and wait time as needed. Add the children's responses to the wall chart.

ASSESS AND **PLAN**   p. Z19

Pictured Words
vase, violin, violets, vest, vine, volcano, vulture, valentine, vacuum cleaner, vanilla

USING THE PICTURE-SORT CARDS

After the illustrations on pages 132 and 133 have been identified and discussed, consider using the *Picture-Sort Cards* for this unit. Possible activities include the following:

▶ Duplicate the *Picture-Sort Cards* for this unit and separate them. Distribute one set of cards to individuals or small groups. Say each pictured word aloud. Ask each student to place the pointer finger of his/her right hand on a *Picture-Sort Card* and then to place the pointer finger of his/her left hand on the matching picture in the illustration in their book. (Students working in groups can take turns.) Walk around to provide assistance and praise their efforts. Encourage children to talk about the pictures.

▶ Separate the *Picture-Sort Cards* and place them in an envelope in an activity center. Label the envelope with the targeted letter, e.g., **V**. Work with individuals or small groups to match each *Picture-Sort Card* with its corresponding picture in the illustration.

For more information on using *Picture-Sort Cards,* see the *Picture-Sort Card Book.*

Diversity in Language and Culture

The \v\ sound is a fricative, which means the sound is made by narrowing the space through which air exits the mouth, creating friction and noise. In the case of \v\, the lower lip curls under the upper teeth, so the sound is called a labiodental fricative. The closest related English sound is \f\. The difference between \v\ and \f\ is that \v\ is voiced—the vocal cords vibrate as the air exits—while \f\ is unvoiced—the vocal cords don't start vibrating until after the sound has started.

Not all languages have the labiodental fricatives \v\ and \f\. Spanish, Japanese, and a number of other languages have bilabial fricatives, which simply means that the lips come close together without closing and without air vibrating between them. The teeth are not involved in producing Spanish \v\ but are used to produce Spanish \f\. Spanish speakers learning English frequently substitute this bilabial sound for the English labiodental sound.

Many speakers of Arabic lack the \v\ sound but use the \f\ sound. Korean has neither \v\ nor \f\.

Children who are missing lower front teeth will temporarily have trouble making these sounds.

HELPING STUDENTS ACQUIRING ENGLISH

Emphasize the *Personal Writing Activities* on page T135 with the students. Here are some suggestions for increasing the effectiveness of these activities with students who are acquiring English.

• Activity A: Students might also write the name of their favorite vegetable in their primary language, or at least write the first letter sound on the page.

• Activity B: Children may substitute an oral explanation in their primary language for what they saw after they have drawn the picture.

• Activity C: The last task of this activity could be modified so students simply label the picture with the name of the object they drew.

• Activity D: Instead of writing an explanation, children might give an oral explanation in English that they have worked out with an English-speaking study buddy.

TEMPORARY SPELLING

(p. 134)

▶ Direct the children's attention to the letter forms at the top of the page.

▶ Demonstrate the formation of capital **V** and lowercase **v**.

▶ Encourage the children to use this page in one of the following ways:

- to practice writing the letter forms;

- to draw one or more pictures of things whose names begin with the same sound as **valentine** and to label each picture;

- to write words that begin with **v**.

▶ Circulate to observe the children's efforts. Ask them to tell you about their drawing and writing.

▶ Accept temporary spellings.

YOUR CHOICE:

 SPELLING PLUS

▶ Invite the children to practice forming **V** and **v** using small valentine hearts or scraps of velvet. Demonstrate the activity.

ASSESS AND **PLAN** p. Z19

V v

PERIOD 4

INTERACTIVE WRITING

▶ Reread "Roses Are Red" aloud.

▶ Write the first two lines of the verse on the chalkboard. Read them again. Ask the children to help you think of two new lines to finish the verse.

▶ Write their responses on chart paper in sentence form. As you write, you may wish to invite the children to tell you the initial letter for words that begin with previously introduced sound-letter relationships (**a** through **v**). (Use your judgment to decide whether this activity is developmentally appropriate for your class at this time.)

YOUR CHOICE:

PERSONAL WRITING

▶ Distribute BLM 22-Valentine. Invite the children to decorate the heart and write a verse on it for a special person in their family or neighborhood.

▶ Encourage temporary spellings.

▶ Allow time for sharing.

ASSESS AND **PLAN** p. Z19

My Writing

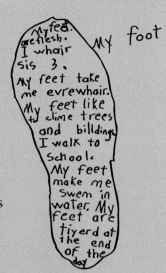

Emergent Spelling Notes

Writing stories using invented spelling helps set the foundations for later spelling competency. This story by Dan includes transitional spelling.

My fee.
areflesh.
I whair
sis 3.
My feet take
me evrewhair.
My feet like
to clime trees
and billdings
I walk to
school.
My feet
make me
swem in
water. My
feet are
tiyerd at
the end
of the
day.

MY foot

Unit 22 **(135)**

PERIOD 5

Getting Ready to Teach

▶ If you choose Activity B, assemble the following materials: clear drinking glass, tablespoon, measuring cup, baking soda, vinegar.

PERSONAL WRITING p. 135

▶ Help the children find page 135.

▶ Choose one of the *Personal Writing Activities* (A–D) listed at the bottom of this page or offer the children a choice.

▶ Accept scribblings, random letters, and invented spellings.

▶ Allow time for the children to share their pictures and writing.

ASSESS AND **PLAN** p. Z19

PERSONAL WRITING ACTIVITIES

Activity A
▶ Discuss vegetables with the children.
▶ Ask them to draw a picture of their favorite vegetable.
▶ Encourage them to label the picture and write something about it.

Activity B
▶ Name the materials you are using and explain what you are doing as you perform the following demonstration: Place a tablespoon of baking soda in the glass. Add a quarter cup of vinegar. (The ingredients will bubble and foam as carbon dioxide is released during the reaction.)
▶ Ask the children to draw a picture of the experiment and write what they observed.

Activity C
▶ Ask the children to write a capital **V** on page 135.
▶ Invite them to draw something that uses the **V** as part of the picture. (For example, the **V** could be a bird's bill or a valley between two volcanoes or the neck of a T-shirt or the pointed end of a carrot.)
▶ Encourage them to write something describing the picture.

Activity D
▶ Write *A Visitor From Venus* on the chalkboard. Read the title and ask the children to write it at the top of page 135.
▶ Ask the children to draw a picture of this visitor from another planet and to write why the visitor has come to Earth.

ADDITIONAL LITERATURE

Carle, Eric. *The Very Busy Spider*. Putnam, 1984.

Modesitt, Jeanne. *Vegetable Soup*. Macmillan, 1988.

Williams, Margery. *The Velveteen Rabbit*. Scholastic, 1988.

GOALS

The children will

▶ develop phonemic awareness.

▶ identify words with the \w\ sound.

▶ associate \w\ with the letter **w**.

▶ engage in interactive writing.

▶ engage in personal writing.

▶ use invented spellings.

MATERIALS

Program materials you will need: student edition pages 136–141, *Assess and Plan File*, BLM 23-Wee Willie Winkie

Optional program materials: BLM 23-Window

Other optional materials: old magazines, scissors, glue, wool yarn

PERIOD 1

Getting Ready to Teach

▶ Copy the poem from page T137 on chart paper.

▶ Cut out the figure on BLM 23-Wee Willie Winkie. Draw 10 to 15 simple houses on the chalkboard. Connect them with a path.

Sharing the Poem (pp. 136–137)

▶ Help the children find pages 136 and 137.

▶ Read the poem to the class, pointing to the words as you read.

▶ Solicit personal responses to the poem. Use these responses and the illustration to guide a brief discussion of the poem.

PHONEMIC AWARENESS

▶ Ask the children to say the word **Willie** with you. Ask them what sound they hear at the beginning of **Willie**. (Response: \w\) Ask if anyone has a name that begins with this sound. (Possible responses: Winona, Wanda, Walter, Wesley)

▶ Read the poem again. Invite the children to raise their hands each time they hear a word that begins with the same sound as **Willie**.

▶ Encourage the children to look around the classroom for things whose names begin like **Willie**. (Possible responses: walls, windows, water, wood, words)

▶ Tell the children they can help Wee Willie Winkie get from house to house by changing the beginning sound in a word you say. Say the word **big**. Ask the children to change the beginning sound to \w\. Model this activity for them by saying **big, wig**. For each response, move Wee Willie Winkie to the next house along the path. Choose words from the following list, modeling additional examples as necessary: **bag (wag), say (way), talk (walk), call (wall), heard (word), fill (will), bear (wear), sent (went), need (weed), rake (wake), good (wood), paste (waste), giggle (wiggle)**.

ASSESS AND **PLAN**   p. Z19

Wee Willie Winkie

Wee Willie Winkie runs through the town,
Upstairs and downstairs, in his nightgown;
Rapping at the window, crying through the lock,
"Are the children in their beds?
Now it's eight o'clock."

Wee Willie Winkie

Wee Willie Winkie runs through the town,
Upstairs and downstairs, in his nightgown;
Rapping at the window, crying through the lock,
"Are the children in their beds?
Now it's eight o'clock."

SOUND-SYMBOL AWARENESS

(pp. 138–139)

▶ Reread "Wee Willie Winkie" to the class.

▶ Write capital **W** and lowercase **w** on a wall chart. Identify the letter and tell the children it stands for the sound they hear at the beginning of **Willie**.

▶ Ask the children to repeat after you first the sound and then the letter several times: \w\, **w**.

▶ Help the children find pages 138 and 139. Ask them if they can find a window in the picture. Write **window** under **Ww** on the chart. Ask them what letter begins the word **window**. (Response: **w**)

▶ Ask the children to find other things in the picture whose names start with the same sound as **window**.

FYI Pictured words are listed at the bottom of the reduced student page.

▶ If you wish to control the naming of the pictured words, ask, *"Do you see a worm?"* and continue in this manner for each pictured word. If you want the children to initiate the naming of the pictures, provide prompts only as necessary.

▶ Write each word on the chart; say the word, emphasizing the beginning sound; and ask the children to repeat it. Ask what letter begins the word.

▶ Ask the children to generate other words that begin with the same sound as **window**. Provide prompts and wait time as needed. Add the children's responses to the wall chart.

 ASSESS AND **PLAN** p. Z19

138 Unit 23

Pictured Words

watermelon, worm, web, watch, window, wagon, water, wasp, walrus, wallet, wing

USING THE PICTURE-SORT CARDS

After the illustrations on pages 138 and 139 have been identified and discussed, consider using the *Picture-Sort Cards* for this unit. Possible activities include the following:

▶ Duplicate the *Picture-Sort Cards* for this unit and separate them. Distribute one set of cards to individuals or small groups. Say each pictured word aloud. Ask each student to place the pointer finger of his/her right hand on a *Picture-Sort Card* and then to place the pointer finger of his/her left hand on the matching picture in the illustration in their book. (Students working in groups can take turns.) Walk around to provide assistance and praise their efforts. Encourage children to talk about the pictures.

▶ Separate the *Picture-Sort Cards* and place them in an envelope in an activity center. Label the envelope with the targeted letter, e.g., **W**. Work with individuals or small groups to match each *Picture-Sort Card* with its corresponding picture in the illustration.

For more information on using *Picture-Sort Cards,* see the *Picture-Sort Card Book.*

Unit 23 **139**

YOUR CHOICE:

 **SPELLING PLUS**

▶ Help the children find page 167.

▶ Ask them to find the letters **Ww.**
Encourage them to draw a picture of
something whose name begins with
w, or provide old magazines from
which they can cut appropriate pictures to glue beside the letters.

▶ You may wish to review words on the
wall chart and suggest the children
choose one of these to illustrate.

Diversity in Language and Culture

This unit focuses on the \w\ sound
spelled **w.** German and a number of
other languages use **w** to stand for \v\.
In French, **w** usually occurs only in
words that have been borrowed from
English or German.

The \w\ sound is complicated to
describe. While it is basically a consonant sound, it shares some characteris-
tics with the **long u** sound and is
sometimes called a semivowel. In producing \w\, the lips are rounded, and
the tongue is pushed back. Some
experts use the term "glide" for the \w\
sound because it always glides into the
following vowel sound.

Many languages do not have \w\.

Some of these languages do have a
sound close to \w\: \oo\ followed by
another vowel. An example from
Spanish is **huevo (egg)** pronounced
\oo-ay-voh\. If you pronounce \oo\ and
glide into \ay\, you will hear what
sounds like \w\. In fact, many experts
say Spanish really does have \w\ in
such words: **huevo** may be pronounced
\way-voh\.

Some learners of English as a second language substitute \v\ for \w\.
Help such speakers to pronounce \oo\
and then glide into the following vowel
sound. Provide practice if the children
need help pronouncing \w\.

**HELPING STUDENTS
ACQUIRING ENGLISH**

Note the information in this unit's *Diversity
in Language and Culture* (on this teacher
page) about **w** in other languages and about
pseudo **w**'s in Spanish (e.g., **huevo**). It is not
surprising, then, that the pictured objects on
pages 138 and 139 do not begin with **w** in
other languages. As a result, there will not
be many sound-alike clues in students' primary languages for this vocabulary.

Ask students to work in groups to write a
story about the illustration, or about an
original idea, using the pictured words on
pages 138 and 139. (You may wish to list
the words in the illustration on the chalkboard before students begin writing.) Ask
groups to share their stories.

TEMPORARY SPELLING

(p. 140)

▶ Direct the children's attention to the letter forms at the top of the page.

▶ Demonstrate the formation of capital **W** and lowercase **w**.

▶ Encourage the children to use this page in one of the following ways:

- to practice writing the letter forms;

- to draw one or more pictures of things whose names begin with the same sound as **window** and to label each picture;

- to write words that begin with **w**.

▶ Circulate to observe the children's efforts. Ask them to tell you about their drawing and writing.

▶ Accept temporary spellings.

YOUR CHOICE:

 SPELLING PLUS

▶ Invite the children to practice forming **W** and **w** using wool yarn. Demonstrate the activity.

ASSESS AND **PLAN**   p. Z19

W w

ASSESS AND **PLAN**   p. Z19

PERIOD 4

INTERACTIVE WRITING

▶ Reread "Wee Willie Winkie" aloud.

▶ Ask the children to recall the things Wee Willie Winkie did in the poem.

▶ Write their responses on chart paper in sentence form. As you write, you may wish to invite the children to tell you the initial letter for words that begin with previously introduced sound-letter relationships (**a** through **w**). (Use your judgment to decide whether this activity is developmentally appropriate for your class at this time.)

YOUR CHOICE:

PERSONAL WRITING

▶ Review the idea that one of the things Willie Winkie did was rap at the windows. Distribute BLM 23-Window. Ask the children to imagine they are looking through this window, either from the inside or the outside.

▶ Invite them to draw what they "see" through the window.

▶ Encourage them to write about what is on the other side of the window.

▶ Encourage temporary spellings.

▶ Allow time for sharing.

My Writing

Emergent Spelling Notes

A precommunicative speller might spell the words on the *Developmental Spelling Test* (page Z6) like this.

1. srysrt
2. dndiin
3. wcsn
4. dwsh
5. rycc
6. wncdn
7. yccr
8. dw
9. snccr
10. hdyc

PERSONAL WRITING   p. 141

▶ Help the children find page 141.

▶ Choose one of the *Personal Writing Activities* (A–D) listed at the bottom of this page or offer the children a choice.

▶ Accept scribblings, random letters, and invented spellings.

▶ Allow time for the children to share their pictures and writing.

ASSESS AND PLAN   p. Z19

PERSONAL WRITING ACTIVITIES

Activity A

▶ Invite the children to draw a winter scene and to write about what they like to do in the winter.

Activity B

▶ Write "I wish..." on the chalkboard. Read the words and ask the children to write them at the top of page 141.

▶ Invite the children to write an ending for the sentence and to illustrate their writing.

Activity C

▶ Discuss different kinds of weather with the children.

▶ Invite them to draw a picture of a particular kind of weather.

▶ Encourage them to label the picture or write something about it.

Activity D

▶ Read *Wombat Stew*. (See *Additional Literature*.)

▶ Invite the children to draw pictures of what they would put into a stew.

▶ Encourage them to label their drawings or write about what their stew tastes like.

ADDITIONAL LITERATURE

Henkes, Kevin. *A Weekend With Wendell.* Penguin Viking/Puffin Books, 1987.

Howell, Lynn, and Richard Howell. *Winifred's New Bed.* Knopf, 1985.

Korth-Sander, Irmtraut (translated by Rosemary Lanning). *Will You Be My Friend?* North-South Books, 1986.

Riggio, Anita. *Wake Up, William!* Atheneum, 1987.

Vaughan, Marcia K. *Wombat Stew.* Silver Burdett, 1986.

G O A L S

The children will

▶ develop phonemic awareness.

▶ identify words with the \ks\ sound.

▶ associate \ks\ with the letter **x**.

▶ engage in interactive writing.

▶ engage in personal writing.

▶ use invented spellings.

M A T E R I A L S

Program materials you will need: student edition pages 142–147, *Assess and Plan File*

Other materials you will need: a jack-in-the-box

Optional materials: old magazines, scissors, glue, ice-cream sticks or tongue depressors, an unmarked box or a box wrapped in plain brown paper

P E R I O D 1

Getting Ready to Teach

▶ Copy the poem from page T143 on chart paper.

Sharing the Poem (pp. 142–143)

▶ Help the children find pages 142 and 143.

▶ Read the poem to the class, pointing to the words as you read.

▶ Solicit personal responses to the poem. Use these responses and the illustration to guide a brief discussion of the poem.

▶ Display a jack-in-the-box for the children to examine.

))))))))) PHONEMIC AWARENESS

▶ Ask the children to say the word **box** with you and to listen for the ending. Ask if anyone has a name that ends like **box**. (Possible responses: Max, Lex, Rex, Tex)

▶ Explain to the children that they can help Jack get out of the box by saying whether a word ends like **box**. For each correct response, allow a child to turn the handle until Jack pops up. Say these words slowly: **fix, pick, fox, cap, mix, sat, six, sock, miss, ax, back, ox**.

◢ **ASSESS** AND **PLAN**   p. Z19

Jack in the Box

Jack in the box all shut up tight,
Not a breath of air,
Not a ray of light.
How tired he must be down in a heap,
We'll open the lid and up he will leap.

—Unknown

SOUND-SYMBOL AWARENESS
(pp. 144–145)

▶ Reread "Jack in the Box" to the class.

▶ Write capital **X** and lowercase **x** on a wall chart. Identify the letter and tell the children it stands for the sound they hear at the end of **box**.

▶ Help the children find pages 144 and 145. Ask them if they can find a box in the picture. Write **box** under **Xx** on the chart. Ask them what letter ends the word **box**. (Response: **x**)

▶ Ask the children to find other things in the picture whose names end with the same sound as **box**.

FYI Pictured words are listed at the bottom of the reduced student page.

▶ If you wish to control the naming of the pictured words, ask, *"Do you see a fox?"* and continue in this manner for each pictured word. If you want the children to initiate the naming of the pictures, provide prompts only as necessary.

▶ Ask the children if they can find something in the picture whose name has the sound **x** stands for in the middle of the word. (Response: **exit**)

▶ Write each word on the chart; say the word, emphasizing the ending sound; and ask the children to repeat it. Ask what letter ends the word.

▶ Ask the children to generate other words that end with the same sound as **box**. Provide prompts and wait time as needed. Add the children's responses to the wall chart.

▶ If the children suggest words that end with **cks,** such as **socks,** write these words in a separate column and explain that in some words \ks\ is spelled **cks.**

YOUR CHOICE:

 SOUND-SYMBOL AWARENESS

▶ You may wish to point out to the children that few words begin with **x**. One they may know is **xylophone**. Write **xylophone** on the chalkboard, read the word, and point out that in **xylophone** the letter **x** represents \z\.

ASSESS AND **PLAN**   p. Z19

Pictured Words
box, fox, ax, six, ox, mix, wax, exit

USING THE PICTURE-SORT CARDS

After the illustrations on pages 144 and 145 have been identified and discussed, consider using the *Picture-Sort Cards* for this unit. Possible activities include the following:

▶ Duplicate the *Picture-Sort Cards* for this unit and separate them. Distribute one set of cards to individuals or small groups. Say each pictured word aloud. Ask each student to place the pointer finger of his/her right hand on a *Picture-Sort Card* and then to place the pointer finger of his/her left hand on the matching picture in the illustration in their book. (Students working in

groups can take turns.) Walk around to provide assistance and praise their efforts. Encourage children to talk about the pictures.

▶ Separate the *Picture-Sort Cards* and place them in an envelope in an activity center. Label the envelope with the targeted letter, e.g., **X**. Work with individuals or small groups to match each *Picture-Sort Card* with its corresponding picture in the illustration.

For more information on using *Picture-Sort Cards,* see the *Picture-Sort Card Book.*

Unit 24 (145)

YOUR CHOICE:

SPELLING PLUS

▶ Help the children find page 168.

▶ Ask them to find the letters **Xx**. Encourage them to draw a picture of something whose name ends with **x,** or provide old magazines from which they can cut appropriate pictures to glue beside the letters.

▶ You may wish to review words on the wall chart and suggest the children choose one of these to illustrate.

Diversity in Language and Culture

The use of **x** to stand for \ks\, the blend it usually represents (except at the beginning of words), goes back to some forms of ancient Greek and Latin.

Only a few words begin with **x,** and no English words begin with \ks\. Words that begin with **x** usually come from Greek. In such words, **x** stands for the same sound as **z,** \z\. The word **xylophone,** which often represents **X** in alphabet books, is from the Greek words **xylon,** meaning "wood," and **phone,** meaning "sound." (A true xylophone has wooden bars.)

The \ks\ blend can be complicated for English language learners. It begins with \k\, which is produced by blocking air at the soft palate, or velum. The air is then released suddenly, and the tongue immediately moves to form the \s\ fricative. This sound is produced by forcing air through the rounded space formed by the tongue. Learners sometimes find this difficult to do. Practice may be needed to make all the necessary movements smoothly.

Be aware that in some varieties of American English, **ask** is pronounced \aks\. While this is not considered standard today, it is actually a very old pronunciation of **ask** and was common in parts of England centuries ago.

HELPING STUDENTS ACQUIRING ENGLISH

Provide students with a copy of the illustration on pages 144 and 145 on legal size paper. (A black-and-white photocopy is fine.) Also provide them with scissors and self-sticking notes. Then ask the students to create small labels with the names of the pictured words and stick them beside the objects they name. Then, working with a study buddy, ask them to point to the words and pronounce them. (Each study buddy should be a student whose first language is English or who has reached a more advanced level of English acquisition.) Ask the study buddy to check to be sure the objects are correctly labeled.

TMPRE **TEMPORARY SPELLING**

(p. 146)

▶ Direct the children's attention to the letter forms at the top of the page.

▶ Demonstrate the formation of capital **X** and lowercase **x**.

▶ Encourage the children to use this page in one of the following ways:

- to practice writing the letter forms;
- to draw one or more pictures of things whose names end with the same sound as **box** and to label each picture;
- to write words that end with **x**.

▶ Circulate to observe the children's efforts. Ask them to tell you about their drawing and writing.

▶ Accept temporary spellings.

YOUR CHOICE:

 SPELLING PLUS

▶ Invite the children to practice forming **X** and **x** using ice-cream sticks or tongue depressors. Demonstrate the activity.

◣ **ASSESS** AND **PLAN**   p. Z19

 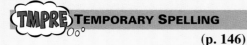

Letters and Words

X x

(146) Unit 24

PERIOD 4

✎ **INTERACTIVE WRITING**

▶ Reread "Jack in the Box" aloud.

▶ Ask the children to recall something the poem says about Jack in the box.

▶ Write their responses on chart paper in sentence form. As you write, you may wish to invite the children to tell you the initial letter for words that begin with previously introduced sound-letter relationships (**a** through **w**). (Use your judgment to decide whether this activity is developmentally appropriate for your class at this time.)

YOUR CHOICE:

✎ **PERSONAL WRITING**

▶ Ask the children to name things that come in a box. (Possible responses: presents, food, cleaning products, crayons, toys, appliances) Invite them to draw a picture of a box and to illustrate the outside of the box.

▶ Encourage them to write a description of what is inside the box.

▶ Encourage temporary spellings.

▶ Allow time for sharing.

◣ **ASSESS** AND **PLAN**   p. Z19

My Writing

PERSONAL WRITING   p. 147

▶ Help the children find page 147.

▶ Choose one of the *Personal Writing Activities* (A–D) listed at the bottom of this page or offer the children a choice.

▶ Accept scribblings, random letters, and invented spellings.

▶ Allow time for the children to share their pictures and writing.

ASSESS AND PLAN   p. Z19

Emergent Spelling Notes

A semiphonetic speller might spell the words on the *Developmental Spelling Test* (page Z6) like this.

1. MSd
2. U N t
3. GaS
4. B t m
5. H t
6. H M N
7. E g l
8. l O Z d
9. B t
10. t i B

Unit 24   (147)

PERSONAL WRITING ACTIVITIES

Activity A

▶ Ask the children to write a capital **X** on page 147.

▶ Invite them to draw something that uses the **X** as part of the picture. (For example, the **X** could be a crossroads or whiskers on a face or part of a fence, a table, or an ironing board.)

▶ Encourage them to write something describing the picture.

Activity B

▶ Ask the children to draw a secret treasure map and mark an **X** to show where the treasure is.

▶ Encourage them to write something about the secret treasure or to write directions for finding the treasure.

Activity C

▶ Read a chapter from *Now We Are Six*. (See *Additional Literature*.)

▶ Invite the children to illustrate the story. Encourage them to retell the story, in writing, in their own words.

Activity D

▶ Display a plain box. Ask the children to think about what might be inside.

▶ Invite them to draw a picture of something that would fit in the box. Encourage them to label the picture or write something about what they imagine is in the box.

ADDITIONAL LITERATURE

McPhail, David. *Fix-It*. Dutton, 1984.

Marshall, James. *Fox on the Job*. Dial Books for Young Readers, 1988.

Milne, A.A. *Now We Are Six*. E.P. Dutton, 1988.

Viorst, Judith. *I'll Fix Anthony*. Harper & Row, 1969.

G O A L S

The children will

▶ develop phonemic awareness.

▶ identify words with the \y\ sound.

▶ associate \y\ with the letter **y**.

▶ engage in interactive writing.

▶ engage in personal writing.

▶ use invented spellings.

M A T E R I A L S

Program materials you will need:
student edition pages 148–153, *Assess
and Plan File,* a photograph of a yak

Optional materials: old magazines,
scissors, glue, yellow yarn, yellow
construction paper, one fresh yam, one
can of yams

P E R I O D 1

Getting Ready to Teach

▶ Copy the poem from page T149 on
chart paper.

Sharing the Poem (pp. 148–149)

▶ Help the children find pages 148 and
149.

▶ Read the poem to the class, pointing to
the words as you read.

▶ Solicit personal responses to the poem.
Use these responses and the illustration
to guide a brief discussion of the poem.

▶ Show the children a photograph of a
yak. Ask them to compare the yak in
the photograph to the ones in their
books.

))))))))) PHONEMIC AWARENESS

▶ Ask the children to say the word **yak**
with you. Ask them what sound they
hear at the beginning of **yak**.
(Response: \y\) Ask if anyone has a
name that begins with this sound.
(Possible responses: Ying, Yoshi,
Yoko, Yolanda)

▶ Read the poem again. Invite the children to raise their hands each time they
hear a word that begins with the same
sound as **yak**.

▶ Tell the children you will say the last
part of a word and you would like them
to say the whole word by adding \y\ to
the beginning. Use these word parts:
am (**yam**), **awn** (**yawn**), **ard** (**yard**),
ear (**year**), **ell** (**yell**), **es** (**yes**), **ou**
(**you**), **oung** (**young**), **ellow** (**yellow**),
esterday (**yesterday**).

▶ **ASSESS** AND **PLAN**   p. Z19

The Yak

Yickity-yackity, yickity-yak,
the yak has a scriffily, scraffily back;
some yaks are brown yaks and some yaks are black,
yickity-yackity, yickity-yak.

Sniggildy-snaggildy, sniggildy-snag;
the yak is all covered with shiggildy-shag;
he walks with a ziggildy-zaggildy-zag,
sniggildy-snaggildy, sniggildy-snag.

Yickity-yackity, yickity-yak,
the yak has a scriffily, scraffily back;
some yaks are brown yaks and some yaks are black,
yickity-yackity, yickity-yak.

—Jack Prelutsky

SOUND-SYMBOL AWARENESS
(pp. 150–151)

▶ Reread "The Yak" to the class.

▶ Write capital **Y** and lowercase **y** on a wall chart. Identify the letter and tell the children it stands for the sound they hear at the beginning of **yak**.

▶ Ask the children to repeat after you first the sound and then the letter several times: \y\, **y**.

▶ Help the children find pages 150 and 151. Ask them if they can find something yellow in the picture. Write **yellow** under **Yy** on the chart. Ask them what letter begins the word **yellow**. (Response: **y**)

▶ Ask the children to find other things in the picture whose names start with the same sound as **yellow**.

FYI ▷ Pictured words are listed at the bottom of the reduced student page.

▶ If you wish to control the naming of the pictured words, ask, *"Do you see some yarn?"* and continue in this manner for each pictured word. If you want the children to initiate the naming of the pictures, provide prompts only as necessary.

▶ Write each word on the chart; say the word, emphasizing the beginning sound; and ask the children to repeat it. Ask what letter begins the word.

▶ Ask the children to generate other words that begin with the same sound as **yak** and **yellow**. Provide prompts and wait time as needed. Add the children's responses to the wall chart.

FYI ▷ You may wish to point out that the leg of the picnic table forms a capital **Y**.

ASSESS AND **PLAN** p. Z19

Pictured Words
yellow, yo-yo, yawn, yolk, yarn, yard, yam, yell

USING THE PICTURE-SORT CARDS

After the illustrations on pages 150 and 151 have been identified and discussed, consider using the *Picture-Sort Cards* for this unit. Possible activities include the following:

▶ Duplicate the *Picture-Sort Cards* for this unit and separate them. Distribute one set of cards to individuals or small groups. Say each pictured word aloud. Ask each student to place the pointer finger of his/her right hand on a *Picture-Sort Card* and then to place the pointer finger of his/her left hand on the matching picture in the illustration in their book. (Students working in groups can take turns.) Walk around to provide assistance and praise their efforts. Encourage children to talk about the pictures.

▶ Separate the *Picture-Sort Cards* and place them in an envelope in an activity center. Label the envelope with the targeted letter, e.g., **Y**. Work with individuals or small groups to match each *Picture-Sort Card* with its corresponding picture in the illustration.

For more information on using *Picture-Sort Cards,* see the *Picture-Sort Card Book.*

Help the children find page 168.

YOUR CHOICE:

SPELLING PLUS

▶ Help the children find page 168.

▶ Ask them to find the letters **Yy**. Encourage them to draw a picture of something whose name begins with **y**, or provide old magazines from which they can cut appropriate pictures to glue beside the letters.

▶ You may wish to review words on the wall chart and suggest the children choose one of these to illustrate.

Diversity in Language and Culture

The letter **y** at the beginning of a syllable stands for a consonant glide (also called a semivowel). In producing \y\, the tongue is pushed forward and up toward the roof (or palate) of the mouth, and the jaw is barely open.

As a glide, \y\ begins with \ee\ and then glides into the vowel that follows, as in **yellow** \ee-eh-loh\.

HELPING STUDENTS ACQUIRING ENGLISH

Ask the students to point out the pictured words in the illustration on pages 150 and 151. Then, ask the students to explain—in their own words in English—what is happening in the illustration. The students may work with a study buddy until they are confident of what they are going to say. (Each study buddy should be a student whose first language is English or a student who has reached a more advanced level of English acquisition.) Listen to each student when he or she is ready. After the oral explanation, ask the student to write down the explanation. Display the written explanations in class.

TEMPORARY SPELLING

(p. 152)

▶ Direct the children's attention to the letter forms at the top of the page.

▶ Demonstrate the formation of capital **Y** and lowercase **y**.

▶ Encourage the children to use this page in one of the following ways:

- to practice writing the letter forms;
- to draw one or more pictures of things whose names begin with the same sound as **yak** and to label each picture;
- to write words that begin with **y**.

▶ Circulate to observe the children's efforts. Ask them to tell you about their drawing and writing.

▶ Accept temporary spellings.

YOUR CHOICE:

 SPELLING PLUS

▶ Invite the children to practice forming **Y** and **y** using yellow yarn. Demonstrate the activity.

 ASSESS AND **PLAN**   **p. Z19**

Letters and Words

Y y

INTERACTIVE WRITING

▶ Reread "The Yak" aloud.

▶ Ask the children to help you write a description of the yak by recalling details from the poem.

▶ Write their responses on chart paper in sentence form. As you write, you may wish to invite the children to tell you the initial letter for words that begin with previously introduced sound-letter relationships (**a** through **y**). (Use your judgment to decide whether this activity is developmentally appropriate for your class at this time.)

YOUR CHOICE:

PERSONAL WRITING

▶ Invite the children to draw a picture of a real or imaginary animal and to write a description of it.

▶ Encourage temporary spellings.

▶ Allow time for sharing.

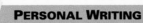 **ASSESS** AND **PLAN**   **p. Z19**

My Writing

Emergent Spelling Notes

A phonetic speller might spell the words on the *Developmental Spelling Test* (page Z6) like this.

1 Mostr
2 uNItd
3 Dras
4 Bottm
5 Hit
6 Ulmn
7 egl
8 cLotSd
9 Bllt
10 tiPt

Unit 25 **153**

PERSONAL WRITING   p. 153

▶ Help the children find page 153.

▶ Choose one of the *Personal Writing Activities* (A–D) listed at the bottom of this page or offer the children a choice.

▶ Accept scribblings, random letters, and invented spellings.

▶ Allow time for the children to share their pictures and writing.

ASSESS AND PLAN   p. Z19

PERSONAL WRITING ACTIVITIES

Activity A

▶ Read "What Is Yellow?" from *Hailstones and Halibut Bones*. (See *Additional Literature*.) Invite the children to name other things that are yellow.

▶ Distribute sheets of yellow construction paper. Invite the children to cut out something that is yellow and glue it on page 153.

▶ Encourage them to label their shapes or to write something about them.

Activity B

▶ Distribute yellow yarn. Invite the children to make a picture with the yarn and glue it on page 153.

▶ Encourage them to write about the yarn picture.

Activity C

▶ Invite the children to draw a picture of something they did yesterday.

▶ Encourage them to label the picture or write a journal entry about yesterday's activities.

Activity D

▶ Display a fresh yam. Invite the children to draw a picture of it.

▶ Invite them to taste canned yams. Encourage them to describe the taste in writing.

ADDITIONAL LITERATURE

Johnston, Tony. *Yonder*. Dial Books for Young Readers, 1988.

O'Neill, Mary. *Hailstones and Halibut Bones*. Doubleday, 1989.

Wolff, Ashley. *A Year of Beasts*. E.P. Dutton, 1986.

G O A L S

The children will

▶ develop phonemic awareness.

▶ identify words with the \z\ sound.

▶ associate \z\ with the letter **z**.

▶ engage in interactive writing.

▶ engage in personal writing.

▶ use invented spellings.

M A T E R I A L S

Program materials you will need: student edition pages 154–159, *Assess and Plan File,* BLMs 26-Zoo 1 and 26-Zoo 2

Optional materials: old magazines, scissors, glue, gummed paper reinforcements

P E R I O D 1

Getting Ready to Teach

▶ Copy the poem from page T155 on chart paper.

▶ Cut out the animal figures on BLMs 26-Zoo 1 and 26-Zoo 2.

Sharing the Poem (pp. 154–155)

▶ Help the children find pages 154 and 155.

▶ Read the poem to the class, pointing to the words as you read.

▶ Solicit personal responses to the poem. Use these responses and the illustration to guide a brief discussion of the poem.

)))) PHONEMIC AWARENESS

▶ Ask the children to say the word **zipper** with you. Ask them what sound they hear at the beginning of **zipper**. (Response: \z\) Ask if anyone has a name that begins with this sound. (Possible responses: Zachary, Zoe, Zeke, Zenobia, Zinnia)

▶ Read the poem again. Invite the children to raise their hands each time they hear a word that begins with the same sound as **zipper**.

▶ Draw a large circle on the chalkboard and write the word **ZOO** above it. Tell the children some animals have escaped from the zoo. Invite them to help return the animals to the zoo by changing the beginning sound in words you say.

▶ Say the word **too**. Ask the children to change the beginning sound to \z\. Model this activity for them by saying **too, zoo**. Use these words: **tip** (**zip**), **rap** (**zap**), **boom** (**zoom**), **dipper** (**zipper**), **hero** (**zero**), **bone** (**zone**), **moo** (**zoo**), **best** (**zest**). For each response, return a picture of an animal to the zoo.

◢ ASSESS AND PLAN   p. Z19

My Zipper Suit

My zipper suit is bunny-brown—
The top zips up, the legs zip down.
I wear it every day.
My daddy brought it out from town.
Zip it up, and zip it down,
And hurry out to play!

—Marie Louise Allen

SOUND-SYMBOL AWARENESS
(pp. 156–157)

▶ Reread "My Zipper Suit" to the class.

▶ Write capital **Z** and lowercase **z** on a wall chart. Identify the letter and tell the children it stands for the sound they hear at the beginning of **zipper**.

▶ Ask the children to repeat after you first the sound and then the letter several times: \z\, **z**.

▶ Help the children find pages 156 and 157. Ask them if they can find a zipper in the picture. Write **zipper** under **Zz** on the chart. Ask them what letter begins the word **zipper**. (Response: **z**)

▶ Ask the children to find other things in the picture whose names start with the same sound as **zipper**.

FYI Pictured words are listed at the bottom of the reduced student page.

▶ If you wish to control the naming of the pictured words, ask, *"Do you see a zero?"* and continue in this manner for each pictured word. If you want the children to initiate the naming of the pictures, provide prompts only as necessary.

▶ Write each word on the chart; say the word, emphasizing the beginning sound; and ask the children to repeat it. Ask what letter begins the word.

▶ Ask the children to generate other words that begin with the same sound as **zipper**. Provide prompts and wait time as needed. Add the children's responses to the wall chart.

ASSESS AND **PLAN**   p. Z19

Pictured Words
zipper, zigzag, zebra, zero, zoo, zither

USING THE PICTURE-SORT CARDS

After the illustrations on pages 156 and 157 have been identified and discussed, consider using the *Picture-Sort Cards* for this unit. Possible activities include the following:

▶ Duplicate the *Picture-Sort Cards* for this unit and separate them. Distribute one set of cards to individuals or small groups. Say each pictured word aloud. Ask each student to place the pointer finger of his/her right hand on a *Picture-Sort Card* and then to place the pointer finger of his/her left hand on the matching picture in the illustration in their book. (Students working in groups can take turns.) Walk around to provide assistance and praise their efforts. Encourage children to talk about the pictures.

▶ Separate the *Picture-Sort Cards* and place them in an envelope in an activity center. Label the envelope with the targeted letter, e.g., **Z**. Work with individuals or small groups to match each *Picture-Sort Card* with its corresponding picture in the illustration.

For more information on using *Picture-Sort Cards,* see the *Picture-Sort Card Book.*

Diversity in Language and Culture

The \z\ sound involves curling the sides of the tongue slightly and bringing the flat part of the tongue up toward the back of the upper front teeth. Air is then forced through the rounded space.

Lisps are common in young children. If the front teeth are missing, the air will travel the same route, but there won't be as much friction because of the open space. The resulting sound will be closer to \th\ than to \z\. Many children who lisp will stop after their front teeth grow in. In some children, the lisp is actually more like a \zh\ sound. This condition is often found in children who have cerebral palsy, and the lisp may not disappear.

The sound most similar to \z\ is \s\, which is produced in the same way as \z\ except that the vocal cords do not vibrate until after the sound begins. If you try to whisper a word with \z\ (such as **zebra**), you will hear a voiceless \s\ instead. Some languages, like Spanish, have only the voiceless \s\ and lack \z\ (as it is pronounced in English words) altogether.

The \z\ sound is less common than \s\ in other languages. A few languages, including Hawaiian, have neither \s\ nor \z\.

If there are children in your class who lisp or have trouble producing \z\ or \s\, model the sounds for them. Realize, however, that some children may not yet be able to produce these sounds correctly. In most cases, the problem will correct itself over time.

HELPING STUDENTS ACQUIRING ENGLISH

Ask students to pretend that they are bees. Have them make a buzzing sound (**zzzzz**) as they walk around pretending to be bees. Explain that they have been making the sound of the letter **z.**

Pronounce the pictured words on pages 156 and 157 with them several times until they understand the connection between the noise they were making and the letter **z** in the words.

Emphasize Activity A (under *Personal Writing Activities*) and the *Your Choice: Review* on page T159 with the students.

TEMPORARY SPELLING

(p. 158)

▶ Direct the children's attention to the letter forms at the top of the page.

▶ Demonstrate the formation of capital **Z** and lowercase **z**.

▶ Encourage the children to use this page in one of the following ways:

- to practice writing the letter forms;
- to draw one or more pictures of things whose names begin with the same sound as **zipper** and to label each picture;
- to write words that begin with **z**.

▶ Circulate to observe the children's efforts. Ask them to tell you about their drawing and writing.

▶ Accept temporary spellings.

YOUR CHOICE:

 SPELLING PLUS

▶ Invite the children to practice forming **Z** and **z** using zeros (or gummed reinforcements to represent zeros). Demonstrate the activity.

◢ **ASSESS** AND **PLAN**   p. Z19

Letters and Words

Z z

PERIOD 4

INTERACTIVE WRITING

▶ Reread "My Zipper Suit" aloud.

▶ Invite the children to tell you something about the zipper suit or the child in the poem.

▶ Write their responses on chart paper in sentence form. As you write, you may wish to invite the children to tell you the initial letter for words that begin with previously introduced sound-letter relationships (**a** through **z**). (Use your judgment to decide whether this activity is developmentally appropriate for your class at this time.)

YOUR CHOICE:

 PERSONAL WRITING

▶ Invite the children to draw a picture of a zipper and to make a list of things that have zippers or to write a description of something they own that has a zipper.

▶ Encourage temporary spellings.

▶ Allow time for sharing.

◢ **ASSESS** AND **PLAN**   p. Z19

My Writing

Emergent Spelling Notes

A transitional speller might spell the words on the *Developmental Spelling Test* (page Z6) like this.

1. monstor
2. younighted
3. dres
4. bottum
5. hicked
6. humun
7. egul
8. clossed
9. bumpped
10. tipe

Unit 26 **159**

PERSONAL WRITING   p. 159

▶ Help the children find page 159.

▶ Choose one of the *Personal Writing Activities* (A–D) listed at the bottom of this page or offer the children a choice.

▶ Accept scribblings, random letters, and invented spellings.

▶ Allow time for the children to share their pictures and writing.

YOUR CHOICE: Review

▶ Use the third and fourth pages of Units 1–25 to review sound-letter relationships. Encourage the children to find the items in each picture whose names begin with the letter shown at the top of the left-hand page.

▶ Pronounce words beginning with the sound-letter relationships you wish to review. Ask the children to name the letter that stands for the beginning sound. Use these words: **rabbit, nurse, boot, panda, quack, foot, water, coat, zoom, ever, inch, gorilla, tunnel, kiss, yesterday, hello, ask, sandwich, ostrich, dance, umbrella, jungle, lamb, monkey, violet.**

 ASSESS AND PLAN   p. Z19

 PERSONAL WRITING ACTIVITIES

Activity A

▶ Read aloud the "Z" section of *Dr. Seuss's ABC* (see *Additional Literature*) without showing the children a picture.

▶ Invite them to draw a picture of a Zizzer-Zazzer-Zuzz.

▶ Encourage them to label the picture or write something about it.

Activity B

▶ Ask the children to write a zero on page 159.

▶ Invite them to draw something that uses the zero as part of the picture. (For example, the zero could be a wheel on a vehicle or an eye in a funny face or the opening to a secret cave.)

▶ Encourage them to write something about the picture.

Activity C

▶ Invite the children to write a folktale about how the zebra got its stripes.

▶ You may wish to have the children work with partners on their stories. Encourage them to illustrate their writing.

Activity D

▶ Read *Z Was Zapped: A Play in Twenty-Six Acts*. (See *Additional Literature*.)

▶ Invite the children to illustrate something in the book.

▶ Encourage them to label their pictures or write something about them.

 ADDITIONAL LITERATURE

Peet, Bill. *Zella, Zack, and Zodiac*. Houghton Mifflin, 1986.

Seuss, Dr. *Dr. Seuss's ABC*. Random House, 1988.

Van Allsburg, Chris. *Z Was Zapped: A Play in Twenty-Six Acts*. Houghton Mifflin, 1987.

FYI These pages may be used to reinforce letter-sound relationships. Instructions for the use of these pages are included in each unit in the teacher edition and repeated here for your convenience.

▶ Help the children find the appropriate letter page.

▶ Ask them to find the appropriate letters on the page. Encourage them to draw a picture of something whose name begins with that letter in the space beside the letter, or provide old magazines from which they can cut appropriate pictures to glue beside the letters.

▶ You may wish to review words on the wall chart and suggest the children choose one of these to illustrate.

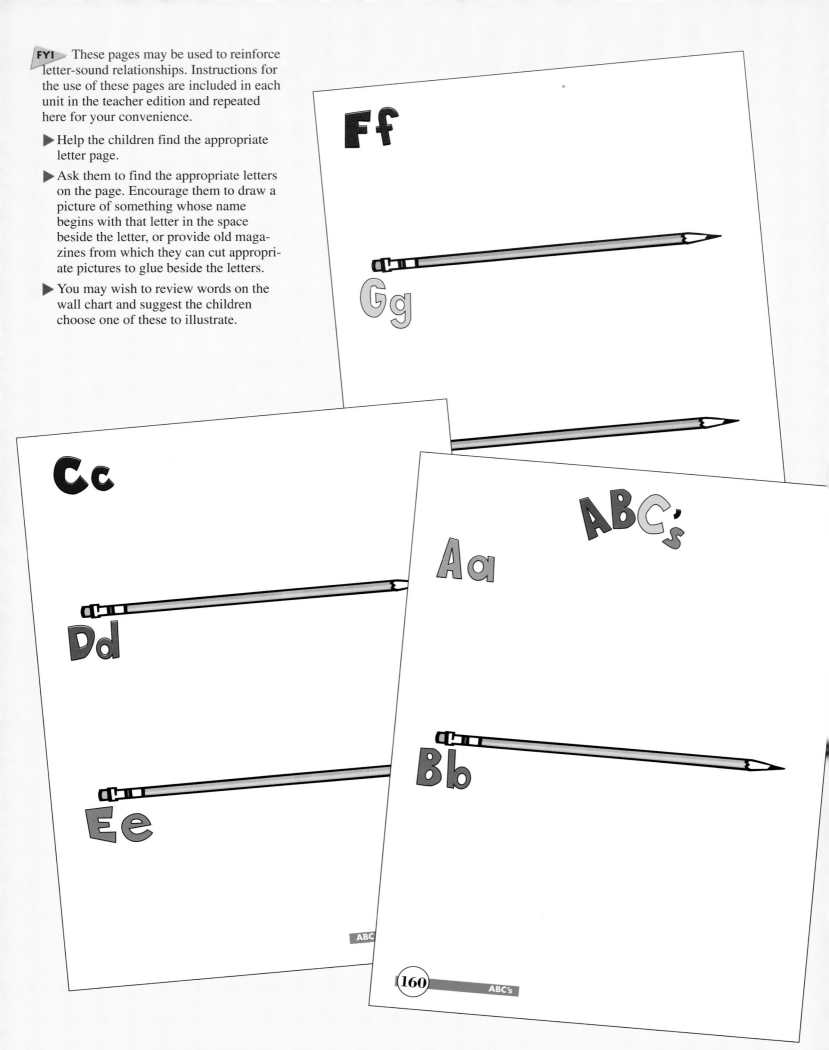

Oo

Ll

Mm

Ii

Nn

Jj

Kk

Xx

Yy

Zz

Uu

Vv

Rr

Ss

Tt

Alphabetical List of Poems

Scope and Sequence

	Grade K	Grade 1	Grade 2
Sound-Symbol Relationships			
Short Vowels			
short a		Unit 12	Units 2, 5
short e		Unit 13	Units 2, 7
short i		Unit 14	Units 2, 10
short o		Unit 15	Units 3, 12
short u		Unit 16	Unit 3
Long Vowels			
long a		Unit 17	Units 5, 6
long e		Unit 18	Units 7, 8
long i		Unit 19	Units 10, 11
long o		Unit 20	Units 12, 13
long u		Unit 21	
r-Controlled Vowels			
ar, or			Units 19, 20
Consonants			
b	Unit 2		
c	Unit 3		
d	Unit 4		
f	Unit 6		
g	Unit 7		
h	Unit 8		
j	Unit 10		
k	Unit 11		
l	Unit 12		
m	Unit 13		
n	Unit 14		
p	Unit 16		
q	Unit 17		
r	Unit 18		Unit 20
s	Unit 19		
t	Unit 20		
v	Unit 22		
w	Unit 23		
x	Unit 24		
y	Unit 25		
z	Unit 26		
k, ck			Unit 21
ll, ss			Unit 28
Consonant Blends			
assorted blends		page T144	
with l			Unit 17
with r			Unit 18
with s			Unit 16
sp		Unit 10	
st		Units 9, 24	

	Grade K	Grade 1	Grade 2
Sound-Symbol Relationships (Cont.)			
Consonant Digraphs			
ch		Unit 11	
ch, sh			Unit 22
sh, th		Unit 25, page T71	
th			Unit 23
Vowels			
a	Unit 1		
e	Unit 5		
i	Unit 9		
o	Unit 15		
u	Unit 21		
Word Families			
ack, at		Unit 4	
ad, ag, am		page T11	
ake		Unit 7	
an, im		Unit 3	
ap		Unit 1	
ay		page T35	
a-consonant-silent e		page T47	
eck, ick, ock, uck, ut		page T29	
ed, eg, em, et		page T17	
eed, eek, eel, een, eet		page T41	
eep, ug		Unit 6	
en, ot		Unit 2	
id, ig, in, ip, it		page T23	
ob, od, op		page T17	
og, ump		Unit 5	
old		Unit 8	
ut, up, ud		page T41	
Phonemic Awareness	pages T4, T8, T10, T14, T16, T20, T22, T26, T28, T32, T34, T38, T40, T44, T46, T50, T52, T56, T58, T62, T64, T68, T70, T74, T76, T80, T82, T86, T88, T92, T94, T98, T100, T104, T106, T110, T112, T116, T118, T122, T124, T128, T130, T134, T136, T140, T142, T146, T148, T152, T154, T158	pages T6, T8, T12, T14, T18, T20, T24, T26, T30, T32, T36, T38, T42, T44, T48, T50, T54, T56, T60, T62, T66, T68, T72, T78, T84, T90, T96, T102, T108, T114, T120, T126, T132, T138, T144, T150, T156, T162, T168	

Scope and Sequence

	Grade K	Grade I	Grade 2
Spelling Strategies			
Check Your Spelling			pages 27, 75
Invented Spelling			pages T15, T67
Problem Spellings			Unit 20
Rhyming Spelling Strategy			Units 4, 27, page 51
Spelling Study Strategy			pages 19, 67, 79, 103, 137
Test Yourself			page 107
Word Structure			
Base Words			Units 29, 30
Compound Words			Unit 31
Doubling Final Consonant			Units 29, 30, pages T129, T133
Dropping Final e			Units 29, 30, pages T129, T133
Inflected Forms			
-ed			Units 25, 29
-ing		Unit 27	Unit 30
Plurals		Unit 26	Unit 26
Syllables		page T162	
Building Vocabulary			
Color Words		Unit 22	
Homophones		Unit 28	Unit 32
Multiple Meanings			page 15
Number Words		Unit 23	
Rhyming Words		pages T132, T138	
Sound Words		page T53	
Word Histories			pages 23, 39, 43, 47, 55, 83, 99, 117, 125, 141
Word Sorting			Units 5, 6, 12, 13, 21, 25, 29, 30
Writing			
Bar Graphs		pages T23, T59	
Class Book		page T71	
Describing a Process Experience		page T71	
Descriptive Writing		pages T11, T17, T23, T35, T41, T47, T59, T65, T76, T82, T88, T94, T130, T148, T160	pages 33, 41, 73, 81, 89, 93, 139

	Grade K	Grade I	Grade 2
Writing (Cont.)			
Directions			pages 37, 53
Drawing and Labeling Pictures		pages T11, T17, T23, T35, T41, T47, T59, T65, T76, T82, T88, T94, T106, T130, T148, T160	
Interactive Writing	pages T8, T14, T20, T26, T32, T38, T44, T50, T56, T62, T68, T74, T80, T86, T92, T98, T104, T110, T116, T122, T128, T134, T140, T146, T152, T158	pages T10, T16, T22, T28, T34, T40, T46, T52, T58, T64, T70, T76, T82, T88, T94, T100, T106, T112, T118, T124, T130, T136, T142, T148, T154, T160, T166, T172	
Invitations		page T28	
Letters			
Apology		page T70	
Friendly		pages T154, T172	
Personal Notes		page T118	
Thank-you Notes		page T29	
Lists		pages T65, T82	pages 25, 45, 49, 53, 65, 77, 85, 89, 93, 97, 101, 105, 109, 119, 127, 131, 135, 143
Notes and Letters			pages 61, 123
Personal Descriptions		page T112	page 109
Personal Writing	Units 1–26		
Poems			
Colors		page T136	
Holiday		page T166	
Number		page T142	
Pets		page T76	
Season		page T166	
Prewriting Activities			pages 33, 41, 81, 85, 89, 93, 97, 101, 105, 119, 143
Questions and Answers			page 57
Reports		page T106	
Rhymes and Jingles		page T53	
Rhyming Words			page 29
Riddles		page T124	
Self-portraits		page T112	
Sensory Words		page T88	

Scope and Sequence

	Grade K	Grade I	Grade 2
Writing (Cont.)			
Sentences		pages T35, T59, T65, T82	
Songs		page T142	
Stories		pages T41, T59, T100	
Titles			page 21
Webbing			pages 115, 123
Proofreading			Unit 14, pages 17, 93
Dictionary Skills			Unit 9
Handwriting			pages 69, 172–175